TENNESSEE WILDLIFE VIEWING GUIDE

Paul Hamel, Author
Laura Mitchell, Project Manager

FALCON PRESS®

Helena, Montana

ACKNOWLEDGMENTS

John Ramey, Forest Supervisor, and Sam Brocato and Reese Scull, Staff Officers, Cherokee National Forest, made this publication possible by providing funding for salary and incidental costs for the project manager's position.

The Tennessee Wildlife Viewing Guide Committee includes: Laura Mitchell, Chairperson; Bob Ford, Tennessee Conservation League and President, Tennessee Ornithological Society; Paul Hamel, Tennessee Department of Environment and Conservation—Ecological Services (currently with USDA Forest Service); Bob Hatcher, Tennessee Wildlife Resources Agency; Larry Nash, U.S. Army Corps of Engineers; John Mechler, Tennessee Valley Authority; Bill Perdue, Monsanto Company; and Jim Widlak, U.S. Fish and Wildlife Service. Each member was instrumental in the development of this guide.

Special thanks to Charlie Tate, John Froeschauer, Bob Fulcher, Charles Norvell, and Bill Troup at the Tennessee Department of Environment and Conservation, Bureau of State Parks, for their contributions to writing, site nominations, and coordination with Parks personnel. David Etnier reviewed written copy and illustrations and contributed many helpful ideas. Jim Byford, Ron Caldwell, Edward W. Chester, Bud Freeman, Kevin Hollingsworth, Padgett Kelley, Mike Kennedy, Jim Layzer, Milo Pyne, and David Vogt also provided technical review. Steve Ahlstedt, Debbie Andreadis, Judith Bartlow, and Chuck Nicholson of the Tennessee Valley Authority conducted site research, and provided many nominations and technical expertise.

Many photographs in this guide are provided courtesy of the Tennessee Department of Tourist Development; thanks to Mark Forester, and also to Jed DeKalb and Murray Lee with State Photo Services.

Jim Cole, USDA Forest Service, offered the support and leadership to get the project off and running. Kate Davies, Defenders of Wildlife, provided coordination and guidance throughout the project. John Grassy, Associate Editor, Falcon Press, provided enthusiasm and skill as editor.

Ken Dubke, Barbara Stedman, Ann Tarbell, and Martha Waldron of the Tennessee Ornithological Society contributed their valuable time and expertise towards site nominations and site evaluation visits.

Delce Dyer, Jim Herrig and Don Lewis contributed time towards copy review and site evaluations. Thanks to Kay Linder, Deborah Patton, and Cindy Smith-Walters for their interest in linking this guide with Project CENTS.

Finally, sincere appreciation is extended to all on-site managers and others who provided nominations, interviews, tours and text reviews.

State Project Manager: Laura Mitchell

Author: Paul Hamel

National Watchable Wildlife Program Coordinator:
Kate Davies, Defenders of Wildlife

Illustrations: Jo Moore

Front cover photo: Black Bear Cub BILL LEA

Back cover photos: Tennessee Coneflowers TONY MYERS
Yellow Warbler JOHN HEIDECKER

This is an exciting time for conservation in Tennessee! From the banks of the mighty Mississippi to the rugged, wind-blown highlands of the Unaka Mountains, our natural heritage is diverse and inviting.

It's a time when Tennessee's Biodiversity Program is getting under way. By taking inventory of natural habitats across the state and then mapping them, we can develop more effective conservation strategies, and incentive programs for landowners to wisely manage their lands.

It's a time of the opening of the Tennessee Aquarium, celebrating rivers and the ecosystems they support, and offering a chance for young and old to better understand our history and to plan our future.

It's a time when Tennessee's twelve-year-old Wildlife Observation Area program is coming into its own. Unique partnerships are being developed between many agencies and organizations across the state.

It's a time when the interagency Protection Planning Committee is working together, devoted to identifying and protecting significant wildlife habitats.

Witness the wonders of thousands of sandhill cranes, a powerful black bear or a tiny Tennessee cave salamander, migrating warblers, thousands of endangered gray bats, tens of thousands of ducks and geese along the Mississippi flyway, or hundreds of wintering bald eagles at Reelfoot Lake.

We invite you to celebrate and to help conserve Tennessee's rich wildlife heritage, on your own or with family or friends—today!

Ned McWherter

Ned McWherter
Governor

CONTENTS

PROJECT SPONSORS

 The FOREST SERVICE, U.S. DEPARTMENT OF AGRICULTURE, manages the resources of the Cherokee National Forest—Tennessee's only national forest—under the concepts of ecosystem management and sustainable multiple use to meet the diverse needs of people. The Cherokee is proud to sponsor this program in order to promote awareness and enjoyment of fish and wildlife on national forest lands. USDA Forest Service, Cherokee National Forest, 2800 N. Ocoee St., Cleveland, TN 37312. (615) 476-9700.

 DEFENDERS OF WILDLIFE is a national nonprofit organization of more than 80,000 members dedicated to preserving the natural abundance and diversity of wildlife and its habitat. A one-year membership is $20 and includes subscriptions to *Defenders,* an award-winning conservation magazine, and *Wildlife Advocate,* an activist-oriented newsletter. To join or for further information, write or call Defenders of Wildlife, 1244 Nineteenth St. NW, Washington, DC 20036. (202) 659-9510.

 The TENNESSEE VALLEY AUTHORITY's mission is to serve our region and nation by leading the way to quality economic growth based on a competitive energy supply, effective management of the Tennessee River system, demonstrated environmental excellence, and innovative partnerships for community development. TVA, Division of Land Management, 400 West Summit Hill Drive, Knoxville, Tennessee, 37902-1499. Phone 1-800-TVA-LAND.

 The DEPARTMENT OF DEFENSE (DoD) is the steward of about twenty-five million acres of land in the United States, many of which possess irreplaceable natural and cultural resources. The DoD is pleased to support the Watchable Wildlife program through its Legacy Resource Management Program, a special initiative to enhance the conservation an restoration of natural and cultural resources on military land. For more information contact the Office of the Deputy Assistant Secretary of Defense (Environment), 400 Army Navy Drive, Suite 206, Arlington, VA 22202-2884.

 The MONSANTO FUND is proud to sponsor the Watchable Wildlife effort. As part of its seven point "Monsanto Pledge" for continuous environmental improvement, Monsanto is working to manage its plant sites to benefit nature. Our nationally recognized plant site at Columbia, Tennessee, which has a 5,000-acre wildlife enhancement area and a 200-acre Monsanto ponds public wildlife observation area, is an excellent example of Monsanto's commitment to corporate environmental responsibility. 800 N. Lindbergh Blvd., St. Louis, MO. (314) 694-4596.

 THE NATIONAL FISH AND WILDLIFE FOUNDATION, chartered by Congress to stimulate private giving to conservation, is an independent not-for-profit organization. Using federally funded challenge grants, it forges partnerships between the public and private sectors to conserve the nation's fish, wildlife, and plants. National Fish and Wildlife Foundation, Bender Bldg., suite 900, 1120 Connecticut Ave. NW, Washington, DC 20036. (202) 857-0166.

THE TENNESSEE DEPARTMENT OF ENVIRONMENT AND CONSERVATION works to conserve significant elements of Tennessee's natural biological diveristy and to provide technical and planning assistance to agencies, communities, and individuals. The BUREAU OF STATE PARKS works to protect and preserve unique examples of natural, cultural, and scenic areas, and to provide quality outdoor experiences through a well-planned and well-managed system of state parks. TDEC, Ecological Services, 8th Flr., L&C Tower, 401 Church St., Nashville, TN 37243-0447 (615) 532-0431. Tennessee State Parks, 7th Flr., L&C Tower, 401 Church St., Nashville, TN 37243-0446, (615) 532-0001.

The TENNESSEE WILDLIFE RESOURCES AGENCY has legal responsibility for the conservation and management of Tennessee's wildlife resources; and for their consumptive and nonconsumptive use, to the degree compatible with desired wildlife protection. Tennessee Wildlife Resources Agency, P.O. Box 40747, Nashville, TN 37204.

The U.S. ARMY CORPS OF ENGINEERS, NATURAL RESOURCES MANAGEMENT BRANCH, provides support to the nation by managing the natural resources at public lakes and waterways in accordance with authorizing legislation and sound management principles. In Tennessee, the corps manages six major lakes which, along with the Nashville District Office, are sponsors of the Watchable Wildlife program to promote awareness and enjoyment of our nation's natural resources. U.S. Army Corps of Engineers, Nashville District, Natural Resources Management Branch, P.O. Box 1070, Nashville, TN 37202. (615) 736-5115.

The U.S. FISH AND WILDLIFE SERVICE, DEPARTMENT OF THE INTERIOR, is proud to be a sponsor of the Tennessee Wildlife Viewing Guide. The agency has a mandate to conserve, protect, and enhance the nation's fish and wildlife and their habitats for the continuing benefit of the American people. The Service is primarily responsible for the management of migratory, freshwater and anadromous fish, protection and recovery of endangered species, enforcement of federal wildlife laws, research, and administration of the national wildlife refuge system and national fish hatcheries. U.S. Fish and Wildlife Service, 446 Neal Street, Cookeville, TN 38501. (615) 528-6481.

The TENNESSEE DEPARTMENT OF TRANSPORTATION (TDOT), plans, designs, constructs, operates, and maintains the State's highway system. TDOT's mission is to provide for the safe and efficient movement of people, goods, and services, while at the same time caring for the environment and natural beauty of Tennessee. TDOT is pleased to support the Wildlife Viewing Guide by installing the binocular logo signs along Tennessee highways. Tennessee Department of Transportation, Suite 700, James K. Polk Building, Nashville, TN 37243-0349. (615) 741-2848.

The NATIONAL PARK SERVICE is charged with administering the units of the National Park System in a manner that protects and conserves their natural and cultural resources for the enjoyment of present and future generations. National Park Service, 75 Spring Street, SW, Atlanta, GA, 30303. (404) 331-4998.

INTRODUCTION

From the continent's largest river to the summits of the highest mountains in the East, Tennessee's natural beauty spans over 500 miles and 500 million years. Stretching across eight distinct geographic regions and enveloping countless unique wildlife habitats, Tennessee's diversity of plants and animals offers unmatched opportunities for wildlife viewing.

Across the Volunteer State, you may encounter creatures ranging from a 600-pound black bear to the tiny seal salamander, one of Tennessee's many indigenous salamanders. Over 5,000 caves have been catalogued in the "karst" landscape, more than any other state. You'll also find the richest variety of freshwater fish in America, and a diversity of freshwater mussel species unmatched in other temperate regions of the world.

Living in a state with a population of over five million people, and more federally-listed endangered species of plants and animals than any other state without a coastline, Tennesseans understand the fragility of their natural resources. This is a place where recognizing the importance of all living things, including those with names we can't pronounce and whose functions we don't yet understand, is becoming an increasing priority.

This viewing guide will lead you to eighty-one of the best publicly-accessible natural areas in Tennessee. Over 100 sites were nominated and evaluated by wildlife biologists and experienced naturalists throughout the state. The sites selected offer the chance to see seasonal concentrations of wildlife and unique or exceptional habitats. Many sites also feature developed facilities and interpretive elements, such as guided nature walks, brochures, and educational displays.

Whether your destination is a free-flowing scenic river, an arid cedar glade, or a wind-blown mountain peak in the clouds, this book can put you on the path to many memorable wildlife viewing experiences. May it also inspire you to support agencies and private organizations working to safeguard Tennessee's rich natural heritage.

THE NATIONAL WATCHABLE WILDLIFE PROGRAM

The Watchable Wildlife Program is part of a long-term initiative to build a new wildlife constituency in addition to the traditional strong support of hunters and anglers. By cultivating public interest in wildlife watching and related activities, Watchable Wildlife aims to transform public interest into public responsibility for developing and financing future conservation efforts.

With publication of this guide, the next step—enhancement of viewing sites—will be getting under way in Tennessee. This will include development of both facilities (trails, viewing blinds and platforms, parking) and interpretive materials and programs. Not every site appearing in the book will feature developed facilities or interpretation at the time of publication. In many cases, however, the process has begun.

This viewing guide is designed to support Tennessee's **Wildlife Observation Area (WOA)** program, initiated in 1981 by the Tennessee Wildlife Resources Agency's Nongame and Endangered Species Program in cooperation with many partners across the state. Currently forty-five sites of variable ownership have received this special designation, many of which are featured in this guide. Look for the **"WOA"** abbreviation at the beginning of each site account. Visitors in the field should look for the blue egret **WOA** logo sign posted at many of the sites featured in this Guide.

In the future, as additional Watchable Wildlife sites are developed in Tennessee, the familiar brown-and-white road signs featuring a binoculars logo will be installed as soon as possible. The Guide represents an introduction to those sites recognized at the time of publication. Viewers are encouraged to recognize and promote wildlife viewing opportunities in lesser-known locations by contacting a professional biologist with the appropriate agency.

In some cases, visitors may find the binoculars sign only at the entrance to a large refuge, national park, or wildlife management area. In this case, please contact the site owner prior to visiting, or (if available) check with staff at a visitor center or office to locate specific viewing opportunities described in the guide.

VIEWING HINTS AND ETHICS

Choose the best season. Learn about patterns of wildlife movements, particularly bird migration. Waterfowl, shorebirds, and raptors are best viewed when they migrate in large numbers through Tennessee in spring and fall. The warmer months are best for songbirds, small mammals, deer, and amphibians. Winter brings large numbers of northern birds, including bald eagles; owls are more frequently heard.

Visit in the morning or evening. The first and last hours of daylight generally offer the best viewing. Many animals feed before the heat of day, or finish their activities before dark. Nocturnal animals are either still awake or preparing for their nighttime movements. The heat of mid-day, especially in summer, tends to offer the poorest viewing.

Use binoculars or spotting scopes. Optical aids can bridge the distance between you and wildlife. Turn your binoculars upside down to create a mini-microscope for closer looks at plants and small creatures. Polarized sunglasses can reduce glare around water and at higher elvations.

Come prepared. Advance preparation can make your trip enjoyable and productive. Check the facilities at each site before visiting—facilities are always noted, using icons, at the bottom of each site writeup in this guide. Always travel with an up-to-date road map; obtain specialized maps of primitive areas ahead of time.

Move slowly and quietly. Noises often scare wildlife. Notice how many more animals you see when you are still. Many birds, frogs, and mammals can be identified by the songs, calls or sounds that they make.

Use field guides. Field guides are essential for positive identification of the many species named in this guide. Obtain local checklists to aid with identification and information about habitats, seasonal abundance, and much more.

Enjoy wildlife from a distance. Be alert for signs of distress or nervous behavior in an animal, and retreat if you detect them. Feeding or touching wildlife is inappropriate. Young wild animals that appear to be alone have not been abandoned; allow them to go their own way. Never approach mother animals with young. Most snake species are harmless, but a few are poisonous and can be dangerous—observe poisonous snakes from a safe distance.

Be patient. Wild creatures, like you, have their particular habits. Wait quietly for animals to enter or return to an area. Give yourself the gift of enough time to allow animals to move within view.

Use a blind. Your car, boat, or canoe can provide good cover for viewing wildlife.

Respect rights of others. Private landowners own about 95% of the state; obtain permission before entering their property. Use designated trails and roads only. Allow others to have a quiet, pleasant experience. Pick up litter and recycle it as you go.

Avoid using audio tapes of owl calls to attract songbirds, especially during breeding season.

HOW TO USE THIS GUIDE

Your wildlife viewing guide contains a wealth of information. Please take a few moments to become familiar with its design and organization:

This guide is divided into three sections, representing the Grand Divisions of Tennessee. Color tabs on page edges allow you to move quickly from one section to the next. Each section opens with a full-color map and a description of the natural characteristics of the region. Major roads, towns, and all viewing sites appear on the maps. The name of each viewing site in the region appears beneath the map.

Each wildlife viewing site features a series of **wildlife icons** at the top of the page. These icons represent wildlife groups most commonly seen at the viewing site. Wildlife icons are labeled on page 12 under the heading, "Featured Wildlife." As you become familiar with these icons, you can quickly reference the wildlife of every site in the book.

The text of each viewing site includes a description and viewing information. The **description** provides a brief overview of the habitats found at each site, and names specific wildlife species to look for. It is followed by **viewing information** that includes additional species, the probability of seeing selected wildlife, and the best months or seasons for viewing. Specific viewing areas within site boundaries are also offered when possible. *NOTES OF CAUTION RELATING TO ROAD CONDITIONS, SAFETY, AREA CLOSURES, AND OTHER RESTRICTIONS APPEAR IN CAPITAL LETTERS.*

Written **directions** are supplied for each viewing site and, in most cases, begin at the closest town to the viewing site. The name of the **closest town** appears beneath the directions—it is the nearest town to the viewing site offering gas, food, and/or lodging. In all cases, viewers should supplement the directions in this guide with an up-to-date road atlas, county road maps, or, in some cases, topographic maps. When traveling to a viewing site, watch for the brown-and-white binoculars sign. These road signs mark the route to a wildlife viewing area.

Ownership refers to the agency, organization or corporation that owns or manages the viewing site. A **phone number** is included and may be used to obtain additional information about the site. If there are several owners, more than one phone number may be listed. See ownership abbreviations below.

Recreational icons appear at the bottom of each site writeup. These icons are labeled on page 13 and provide important information about recreational opportunities at the viewing site, as well as information on parking, restrooms, and entrance fees.

SITE OWNER/MANAGER ABBREVIATIONS

USFS	USDA Forest Service
TDEC/BPR	Tennessee Dept. of Environment and Conservation/ Bureau of Parks and Recreation
TDEC/SRP	Tennessee Dept. of Environment and Conservation/ Scenic River Program
TDF	Tennessee Division of Forestry
TWRA	Tennessee Wildlife Resources Agency
USFWS	U.S. Fish and Wildlife Service
PVT	Private ownership
TVA	Tennessee Valley Authority
NPS	National Park Service
USACOE	U.S. Army Corps of Engineers
USAF	U.S. Air Force

A WORD ABOUT CAVES

Tennessee's caves are a great natural resource. Although Tennessee has identified more caves than any other state, few caves are featured as viewing sites. This is because caves and cave wildlife are very sensitive. In addition, caves may be dangerous for unprepared or uninformed visitors. Numerous commercial cave tours are listed through most tourist information centers, and some parks and organizations offer guided tours of selected wild caves.

If you own a cave, remember that the land surface is closely linked with the cave habitat and watershed underground. Cave wildlife can be affected by restricting air or water flow underground, by the addition of brush, hay, and other organic materials into the cave, and by contruction of buildings, wells, septic tanks, petroleum tanks, and landfills above ground. Remember, water knows no boundaries in the "karst" terrain of Middle Tennessee.

To learn more about this resource and about cave safety and responsibility, contact the National Speleological Society or a local grotto.

Note: The TWRA toll-free numbers are available for in-state callers only. The toll-free TVA phone number (1-800-TVA-LAND) serves both in-state and out-of-state callers.

FEATURED WILDLIFE

Songbirds/
Perching Birds

Waterfowl

Upland
Birds

Wading
Birds

Birds of
Prey

Marine
Birds

Shorebirds

Hoofed
Mammals

Carnivores

Small
Mammals

Fish

Reptiles
Amphibians

Freshwater
Mammals

Bats

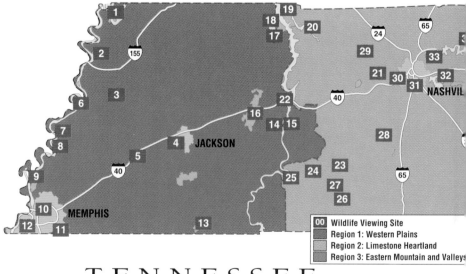

Insects

Wildflowers

TENNESSEE
Wildlife Viewing Areas

FACILITIES AND RECREATION

Parking

Restrooms

Barrier-free

Lodging

Restaurant

Camping

Picnic

Boat Ramp

Large Boats

Small Boats

Hiking

Bicycling

Cross-country skiing

Entry Fee

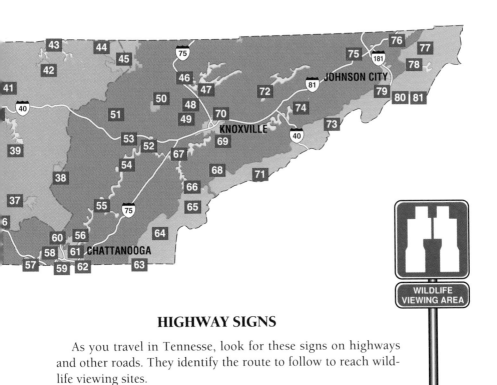

HIGHWAY SIGNS

As you travel in Tennessee, look for these signs on highways and other roads. They identify the route to follow to reach wildlife viewing sites.

WESTERN PLAINS

Reelfoot Lake.   RUSS GUTSHALL

The Western Plains region includes the Mississippi River Valley, the Western Valley of the Tennessee River, and, wedged between these rivers, the Coastal Plain of an ancient sea (see map below). Averaging less than 400 feet above sea level, these rolling hills and flat lowlands are dotted with mounds and bluffs of wind-blown silt called "loess." Histori cally, the land has been shaped by the fluctuating water levels of ancient seas, the continual meandering and flooding of the Mississippi and Tennessee rivers, and the seismic activities of the New Madrid fault, one of the most active in the country. The ongoing effects of these natural forces make the western third of Tennessee, in geological terms, the state's "youngest" region.

The natural cycles of change have been greatly influenced by human inhabitants over time. A series of levees, dikes and navigation structures have altered wildlife habitat along the Mississippi River. Today only Lauderdale County's floodplain is subject to the natural rise and fall of the river. Many of West Tennessee's rivers have

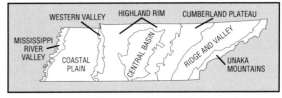

been channelized, or straightened, further modifying wetland and riverine habitats. Meeman Shelby Forest State Park (site 9) and the Hatchie River (site 5) are outstanding remnants of unmodified ecosystems found in the Western Plains today.

Lying within the heart of the Mississippi flyway, broad swampy bottoms host a tremendous influx of migrating and wintering songbirds, waterfowl, and birds of prey. There is a spectacular annual arrival of migrating bald eagles at Reelfoot, Tennessee's largest natural lake. Concentrations of gadwall, mallards, pintails, and Canada geese at Reelfoot and other locations are equally impressive.

Red-eared sliders   STATE OF
TENNESSEE: TOURIST DEVELOPMENT

West Tennessee's rich bottomlands support humid hardwood and bald cypress forests, as well as an extensive soybean and cotton agriculture. Protected green corridors and isolated wetlands harbor great concentrations of wildlife. Enormous numbers of insects produced here provide the foundation for a complex food web that involves a variety of fish, amphibians, and reptiles, as well as aquatic mammals like beaver and otter, and large predators like coyotes and bobcats. The ongoing struggle to balance agriculture and other land uses with the conservation of forested wetlands is a prominent environmental theme of the Western Plains.

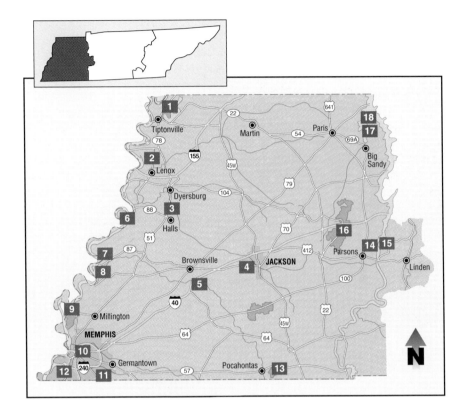

Wildlife Viewing Sites

1 Reelfoot Lake
2 Great River Road
3 Lauderdale Waterfowl Refuge
4 Cypress Grove Nature Park
5 Hatchie National Wildlife Refuge
6 Chickasaw National Wildlife Refuge
7 Fort Pillow State Historical Area
8 Lower Hatchie National Wildlife Refuge
9 Meeman-Shelby Forest State Park and Shelby
    Forest Wildlife Management Area
10 Overton Park
11 Lichterman Nature Center
12 EARTH Complex
13 Big Hill Pond State Park
14 Tennessee National Wildlife Refuge: Busseltown Unit
15 Lady Finger Bluff TVA Small Wild Area
16 Natchez Trace State Park, State Forest, WMA
17 Sam Nickey Wildlife Area
18 Tennessee National Wildlife Refuge: Big Sandy Unit

1 REELFOOT LAKE

Description: WOA. Crown jewel of West Tennessee's natural areas, 33,000-acre Reelfoot Lake area offers spectacular year-round wildlife viewing in a setting of haunting beauty. Extensive bottomland forests, marshes, and bald cypress swamps rim this lake, formed during the violent New Madrid earthquakes of 1811-1812. Habitats attract river otter, white-tailed deer, beaver, coyote, as well as the great blue heron, great and cattle egret, and songbirds in profusion. Hundreds of bald eagles winter here, with peak numbers occurring December through February; look for them perching along the lakeshore, or following commercial fishermen. A smaller number of eagles are year-round residents. This lake may also attract hundreds of thousands of wintering ducks and geese, including mallards, gadwall, American wigeons, and pintails. Shorebird species to watch for include the semipalmated plover, marbled godwit, and pectoral sandpiper—scan the mudflats in spring and early fall. Nesting colonies of great blue herons and great egrets become active in spring. This reputed "Turtle Capital of the World" also features thousands of sliders, stinkpots, and mud and map turtles.

Viewing Information: View from roads, foot trails, and by boat. The Reelfoot Lake area is managed cooperatively by USFWS (Reelfoot National Wildlife Refuge); TWRA (Reelfoot Wildlife Management Area); and TDEC/BPR (Reelfoot Lake State Park). Access information available from each office. Eagle viewing best December through February. Eagle tours offered daily at State Park December through February; pontoon boat tours offered spring through fall—check with visitor center for details. Reelfoot National Wildlife Refuge offers staffed visitor center (open weekdays, also weekends mid-January through mid-April), driving tours through Grassy Island Unit, two observation towers, a self-guided hiking trail, checklists, and brochures. Wildlife Management Area accessed by system roads; maps are available. White-tailed deer and wild turkeys may be seen year-round; shorebirds spring and fall; graceful Mississippi kites soar May through August. Birding excellent year-round. *USE CAUTION DURING HUNTING SEASONS IN APRIL, FALL, AND WINTER IN TWRA'S WILDLIFE MANAGEMENT AREA AND THE NATIONAL WILDLIFE REFUGES. RESPECT POSTED SEASONAL SANCTUARY CLOSURES, TYPICALLY NOVEMBER - FEBRUARY. FEES FOR SOME ACTIVITIES.*

Directions: *From Union City, travel fourteen miles south on TN 22 to TN 157. Turn right, travel one mile to USFWS headquarters/visitor center. From junction of TN 22 and TN 157, continue eight miles south on TN 22 through Samburg, to TWRA headquarters on right. From Tiptonville, drive 2.6 miles east on TN 21/22 to state park visitor center on left.*

Ownership: TDEC/BPR (901) 253-7756; TWRA (901) 253-7343, 423-5725; (800) 372-3928; USFWS (901) 538-2481

Size: More than 33,000 acres   **Closest Town:** Tiptonville, Samburg

Description: This stretch of scenic highway provides an overview of land uses along the Mississippi floodplain—agriculture, forestry, and undrained wetlands. Watch for huge flocks of wading birds, including cattle and great egrets, little and great blue herons, also black-crowned and yellow-crowned night herons; best viewing May through September. Shorebirds such as yellowlegs, the pectoral sandpiper, killdeer, and black-bellied plover appear during migration in May and September. Red-winged blackbirds and dickcissels abundant in summer; red-tailed hawks and northern harriers are abundant year-round.

Viewing Information: For optimal viewing, take this tour during early morning when traffic is minimal and wildlife activity greatest. White-tailed deer, coyote, and raccoon may be seen year-round. Watch for wading birds along forested areas on west side of the road in summer. Sighting a rare fish crow, least tern, or Mississippi kite is possible along this entire route. Waterfowl are abundant in winter fields when floodwaters are high. Road is public, bordered by private lands. *PLEASE RESPECT THE RIGHTS OF PRIVATE LANDOWNERS.* Southern end of road accesses Moss Island Wildlife Management Area, open to public and featuring such wildlife as breeding prothonotary warblers, cottonmouth moccasins, gray squirrels, and wild turkey. Waterfowl are likely in early spring. View from roads or along Willow Flat Lake and Rhoades Lake. *USE CAUTION DURING HUNTING SEASONS AT MOSS ISLAND; INQUIRE AT OFF-SITE TWRA OFFICE.*

Directions: *Access from exit 2 (Great River Road) on Interstate 155 near Lenox. Travel south on TN 181 for 12.3 miles, left on gravel road to Moss Island Wildlife Management Area; reverse to return. Or, travel thirty-four miles north to Kentucky state line via TN 181 north, TN 79 east, TN 78 north. Northern route skirts Reelfoot Lake (Site 1).*

Ownership: PVT; Moss Island managed by TWRA (901) 423-5725; (800) 372-3928
Size: Forty-six-mile drive; Moss Island 3,400 acres
Closest Town: Tiptonville, Dyersburg

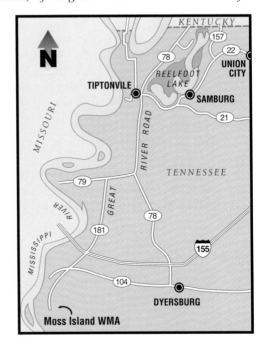

Moss Island WMA

17

3 LAUDERDALE WATERFOWL REFUGE

Description: WOA. Formerly a forested bottom of the South Fork Forked Deer River, this site is an historically important winter feeding and resting area for tens of thousands of waterfowl of the Mississippi River flyway. The wet cropland supports Canada and snow geese, mallards, black and ring-necked ducks, pintails, blue- and green-winged teal, and hooded mergansers; best viewing is mid-October through January. Rare, occasional tundra swans in winter. Warm season wildlife includes wetland mammals, shore and marsh birds, coyotes, and white-tailed deer, not easily observed.

Viewing Information: A spotting scope is a must for optimal viewing here. A highly seasonal site. View only from observation tower. Site is open Nov. 1 through Feb. 15, Sunday-Tuesday, Thursday, and Saturday 7:00 AM - 5:00 PM. Passing trains are occasional disturbance. *ENTIRE AREA IS A REFUGE; NO PUBLIC ACCESS TO HOLDING AREA.*

Directions: *From US 51, take Halls exit onto TN 88 West. Travel 1.6 miles towards Halls, turn left on TN 210. Travel north 2.5 miles to observation tower and small gravel parking area beside railroad on east side of road.*

Ownership: TWRA (901) 423-5725; (800) 372-3928
Size: 690 acres   **Closest Town:** Halls

4 CYPRESS GROVE NATURE PARK

Description: WOA. Visitors here can enjoy close-up views of prothonotary warblers, cottonmouth moccasins, the clay "chimneys" formed by crayfish, and barred owls from a 4,000-foot-long boardwalk winding through humid tupelo and bald cypress forest, and clusters of blue flag iris. These wetlands of the Forked Deer River attract great egrets, belted kingfishers, muskrats, white-tailed deer, and an occasional river otter. Watch for snapping turtles.

Viewing Information: High probability of viewing wetland songbirds, including yellow-throated and prothonotary warblers, and common yellowthroats April through August. Moderate to high probability of seeing barred owls, white-tailed deer, beavers and red-shouldered hawks year-round. Visitor center offers public programs, including guided tours, with advance appointment. Two viewing blinds on site. Raptor rehabilitation facility being developed.

Directions: *From Interstate 40 in Jackson, take US 45 South Bypass exit. Travel 3.5 miles and turn right (west) on US 70 (Airways Boulevard). Travel two miles to entrance sign on left.*

Ownership: City of Jackson Recreation & Parks Department (901) 424-1472
Size: 165 acres   **Closest Town:** Jackson

Description: Red-shouldered hawks and barred owls glide over this refuge, hunting in daily shifts. Bowfin, largemouth bass, and gar fish roil the waters of the adjacent Hatchie State Scenic River, also a stronghold for river otters. The bottomland forest and meandering river channel—the only truly wild tributary remaining in the lower Mississippi River system—provide outstanding habitat for fifty species of mammals, including the raccoon and elusive bobcat. Exceptional numbers of nesting prothonotary warblers, Acadian flycatchers, and American redstarts. Flooded forests shelter wintering mallards, black ducks, and American wigeons. Shorebirds feed on mudflats in spring. Summer heat warms baby hooded mergansers and wood or "summer" ducks as white-tailed deer prepare for fall rut. Watch for swamp rabbits resting on high ground during the flood season.

Viewing Information: View primarily from roads. *INQUIRE AT REFUGE HEADQUARTERS ABOUT ROAD CONDITIONS BEFORE VENTURING INTO BOTTOMLANDS DURING WINTER AND SPRING. USE CAUTION DURING HUNTING SEASON LATE AUGUST-OCTOBER. SOME AREAS CLOSED TO PUBLIC ACCESS NOVEMBER 15-MARCH 15; CHECK AT HEADQUARTERS. DAYLIGHT USE ONLY.* Brochures and maps available at refuge headquarters. Try a float trip from the Big Eddy boat ramp to just west of the TN 76 bridge— fourteen river miles. A brochure of State Scenic River access points is available from TDEC office, off-site. *WEAR SAFETY FLOTATION AT ALL TIMES ON RIVER.*

Directions: *From Interstate 40 near Brownsville, take exit 56. Travel south on TN 76 for 0.25 mile to refuge headquarters on east side of highway. Powell Road/ Windrow Road auto tour parallels Hatchie River through diverse habitats.*

Ownership: USFWS (901) 772-0501; TDEC/SRP (615) 532-0034
Size: 11,556 acres   **Closest Town:** Brownsville

The river otter is making a strong comeback in west Tennessee, thanks to wetland protection efforts at the Hatchie National Wildlife Refuge and other locations. Spectacular athletes on land and especially in water, their bodies are like flexible, streamlined torpedoes. BILL LEA

BOUNTIFUL FORESTS: WETLANDS OF THE WESTERN PLAINS

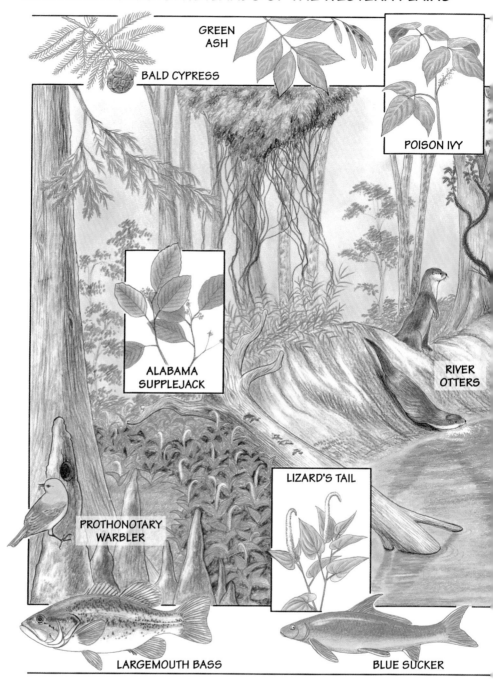

GREEN ASH

BALD CYPRESS

POISON IVY

ALABAMA SUPPLEJACK

RIVER OTTERS

PROTHONOTARY WARBLER

LIZARD'S TAIL

LARGEMOUTH BASS

BLUE SUCKER

Wide rivers meander slowly across the level plains of West Tennessee, bounded by floodplain forests that churn with floodwaters in early spring. As flooding subsides, these forested wetlands come alive with the calls of frogs, the hum of insects, and splashing river otters and bass. Burrowing mussels and worms thrive in the soft, muddy bottom. Turtles and watersnakes bask on every log.

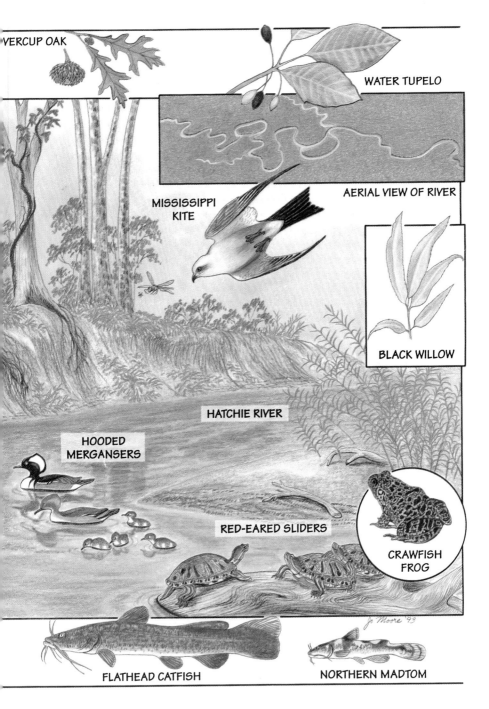

VERCUP OAK

WATER TUPELO

AERIAL VIEW OF RIVER

MISSISSIPPI KITE

BLACK WILLOW

HATCHIE RIVER

HOODED MERGANSERS

RED-EARED SLIDERS

CRAWFISH FROG

FLATHEAD CATFISH

NORTHERN MADTOM

Jo Moore '93

Healthy forested wetlands are valuable to wildlife in many ways. Both fallen and cavity-prone trees provide homes for hooded mergansers, owls, raccoons, and songbirds. Forested wetlands trap sediment, keeping downstream rivers clear. Forested wetlands link habitats, forming travel routes for wildlife. Outstanding examples of forested wetlands may be seen at sites 1, 5, and 9 in this guide.

6 CHICKASAW NATIONAL WILDLIFE REFUGE

Description: Chickasaw National Wildlife Refuge is nestled in the fertile bottomlands of the Mississippi River, its humid forests subject to the annual rise and fall of the this great river. Forests and managed fields provide important habitat in the surrounding "sea" of agriculture.

Viewing Information: Winter concentrations of waterfowl occur at northeast corner of refuge, along the base of Chickasaw Bluff. *SANCTUARY CLOSED TO PUBLIC NOVEMBER 15 - MARCH 15;* during this time, use a spotting scope to view from headquarters compound. During open months, cross gate and walk along a three-mile loop road. Watch for northern shoveler, pintail, Canada and snow geese, and blue- and green-winged teal in winter. Shorebirds visit during spring and fall migrations. Bald eagles may be seen in winter; wild turkey year-round. Abundant white-tailed deer and freshwater mammals. Also watch for great blue and little blue herons, great egrets, and the occasional anhinga. Beautiful view of forested floodplain from TN 19 atop the bluff, looking northwest, is also a reminder of historical habitat conditions in Tennessee. Contact office (on-site) for map of area.

Directions: *From US 51 north of Ripley, take Halls exit and turn left (west) on TN 88. Immediately turn left onto Edith-Nankipoo Road and travel 7.1 miles. Steep downhill section drops off Chickasaw Bluff onto the floodplain. Turn right onto gravel Sand Bluff Road and travel 1.5 miles to trailer headquaters, staffed weekdays.*

Ownership: USFWS (901) 635-7621
Size: 1,426 acres sanctuary; 22,000 acres
National Wildlife Refuge
Closest Town: Ripley

Acrobatic least terns flutter over islands and sandbars of the Mississippi River, diving repeatedly into shallow water for small fish. These endangered birds receive monitoring and management attention from both federal and state agencies and conservation volunteers. A. CRUICKSHANK/VIREO

7 FORT PILLOW STATE HISTORICAL AREA

Description: WOA. Wild turkeys abound at this site, as do white-tailed deer and gray and fox squirrels. Mississippi kites pursue mosquito-hawks and dragonflies on warm summer afternoons. Lines of hungry herons straggle across morning skies. Extensive floodplain and bluff-top forests here provide nesting sites for Acadian flycatchers, Kentucky warblers, northern parulas, yellow-billed cuckoos, and wood thrushes. Bluffs of wind-blown soils offer easy burrowing for small mammals.

Viewing Information: View a wide array of songbirds during spring and fall migrations, and during morning hours in summer. Abundant swallows in July and August. Coyote, bobcat, raccoon, and barred owl are present, but more difficult to see. Scan ponds for painted, mud, and snapping turtles, also red-eared sliders. Trails, general information available at modern visitor center.

Directions: *From US 51 north of Covington, turn left (west) on TN 87 and travel seventeen miles. Turn right (north) on TN 207 at park entrance. Proceed 1.3 miles to visitor center, 3.7 miles to historical interpretive center.*

Ownership: TDEC/BPR (901) 738-5581
Size: 1,000 acres **Closest Town:** Henning

8 LOWER HATCHIE NATIONAL WILDLIFE REFUGE

Description: Managed wet cropland and small remnants of bottomland forest offer a wildlife oasis in surrounding extensive agricultural development. View wading birds along cypress-rimmed ponds spring through fall. Flocks of bobolinks frequent fields atop a bluff bordering the Mississippi River during spring and fall migration. Endangered least terns nest on river sand bars.

Viewing Information: Spectacular swallow flights occur along the river in August. Watch for Mississippi kites over forested eastern portion of refuge on windy spring or summer mornings. Little wildlife activity apparent here during mid-day hours in summer. Waterfowl abundant in winter; a spotting scope is recommended. Best viewing from system roads or boat/canoe. *CONTACT OFF-SITE USFWS OFFICE FOR MAP PRIOR TO VISITING REFUGE. WATER-FOWL SANCTUARY CLOSED TO PUBLIC ACCESS NOVEMBER 15-MARCH 15.*

Directions: *From junction of US 51 and TN 87 near Henning, travel west approximately twenty miles on TN 87. Refuge entrance is on left. Continue about one-half mile to sanctuary, bearing left at a fork in dirt road.*

Ownership: USFWS (901) 538-2481
Size: 500-acre sanctuary; 4,346-acre refuge
Closest Town: Henning

9 MEEMAN-SHELBY FOREST STATE PARK AND WMA

Description: Meeman-Shelby's unbroken forests represent each of the original ecosystems found along the Mississippi Alluvial Plain. Large numbers of wild turkey, white-tailed deer, and raccoon inhabit this area year-round. Endangered least terns nest on islands in the river and may easily be seen from the bank. Sloughs nurture warmwater fishes, a prime food source for water snakes, river otters, and wading birds. Crayfish tempt barred owls and wading birds to dine. Near the edge of their range, Kentucky warblers and Acadian flycatchers are present in great numbers. Migratory warblers in spring. The rare banded whitelip snail reaches the southernmost limit of its range here, and cleans the forest floor. Excellent springtime wildflowers on bluffs of wind-blown soils.

Viewing Information: Information at Visitor Center or Nature Center. View from Chickasaw Bluff Trail, boat launch on Mississippi River, or auto tours. A consistent site for viewing the Swainson's warbler and Louisiana waterthrush during summer nesting. Look for waterfowl in winter. Least terns, wading birds, and Mississippi kites present in summer. Listen for fish crows at developed recreation areas. *USE CAUTION, WEAR BLAZE ORANGE DURING HUNTING SEASON; INQUIRE ABOUT DATES AND LOCATIONS. RESPECT CLOSURES OF SPECIFIED AREAS. SOME ROADS IN BOTTOMS FLOOD DURING SPRING.*

Directions: *From Memphis, travel north on TN 51 to North Watkins Street. Turn left (west) and travel nine miles to Locke Cuba Road. Turn left and proceed 0.75-mile to Bluff Road. Turn right and continue one mile to park entrance and visitor center on left.*

Ownership: TDEC/BPR (901) 876-5201 or (901) 876-5215; managed in cooperation with TWRA (901) 423-5725; (800) 372-3928

Size: 14,000 acres **Closest Town:** Millington

Barred owls are especially abundant in extensive swamp forests. Identified by their dark brown eyes and a barred pattern across the upper chest, they are best known for their loud, rhythmic call of "who-cooks-for-you, who-cooks-for-you-all."

W. GREENE/VIREO

10 | OVERTON PARK

Description: *URBAN SITE.* A landmark U.S. Supreme Court decision on the routing of Interstate 40 spared this wildlife oasis of old growth forest in urban Memphis. Magnificent tulip poplar and red oak trees shelter northern parulas and black-throated green, Tennessee, and hooded warblers during their spring and fall migrations. Nesting Mississippi kites, fish crows, hairy woodpeckers, and white-breasted nuthatches coexist with such urban species as house sparrows, starlings, and rock doves. Watch for albino raccoons. Rich forests feature pawpaw, spring wildflowers, and ferns, along with non-native plants.

Viewing Information: Old growth forest in northeastern corner of park. High probability of viewing migratory songbirds such as scarlet tanager and veery spring and fall; morning hours most productive. *MEMPHIS POLICE ADVISE VISITING IN SMALL GROUPS DURING DAYLIGHT HOURS ONLY, FOR GREATER ENJOYMENT AND PERSONAL SAFETY.*

Directions: *Located in downtown Memphis. Access from East Parkway between Poplar Avenue (US 72) and North Parkway, near picnic area.*

Ownership: City of Memphis, Memphis Park Commission (901) 325-5759
Size: 160 acres of forest; 342-acre park   **Closest Town:** Memphis

11 | LICHTERMAN NATURE CENTER

Description: *WOA/URBAN SITE.* A wildlife oasis, this site's forests, marshlands, and water lily-rimmed pond shelter more than 350 varieties of plants, 200 bird species, forty-five species of reptiles and amphibians, and over thirty species of mammals. Look for more than twenty butterfly species, from the American painted lady to zebra swallowtail, in the center's butterfly garden.

Viewing Information: An extensive self-guided trail system leads to a freshwater marsh, home to belted kingfishers, raccoons, muskrats, and spring peepers. Red-eared sliders, cooters, and other turtles occupy prized sunning spots in the pond year-round. Watch the aerial acrobatics of Mississippi kites May through August. Interpretive center offers brochures and exhibits. Boardwalk, observation deck, paved trails, many activities. Site receives heavy use by school groups weekday mornings in October, November, April, and May.

Directions: *From Interstate 240 loop in east Memphis, take Germantown/Poplar Avenue East exit; travel east on Poplar Avenue several blocks, turning right onto Ridgeway Road. Travel several blocks to Quince Road, turn right, and continue about one-third mile to entrance of Nature Center on right.*

Ownership: City of Memphis (901) 767-7322
Size: Sixty-five acres **Closest Town:** Memphis

12 EARTH COMPLEX

Description: The moist soil and rich invertebrate life at this solid waste disposal site, wastewater treatment and recycling center create ideal manmade habitat for a wonderful variety of birdlife, including nesting black-necked stilts. The 256 bird species recorded here include the state's only known population of painted buntings. Endangered least terns, and shorebirds such as the stilt sandpiper, semipalmated plover, and least sandpiper feed along the edges of wastewater sludge ponds. Watch for mink, muskrat, and beaver in the sloughs of the wildlife sanctuary, in southern portion of area. Adjacent T.O. Fuller State Park offers forests inhabited by cottontail and swamp rabbit, raccoon, skunk, coyote, banded water snake, and the bird-voiced treefrog.

Viewing Information: Excellent birding year-round; bird checklist available. Best viewing for black-necked stilts during nesting period, May through July. Also watch for green-backed herons in summer. Shorebirds abundant during migration spring and fall. Moderate probability of seeing muskrat and beaver year-round. *ROAD SYSTEM CHANGES OFTEN, MAY BE MUDDY FOLLOWING HEAVY RAINS. PLEASE STOP AT OFFICE FOR INFORMATION ON ROAD CONDITIONS AND DIRECTIONS TO BEST VIEWING AREAS. USE BINOCULARS OR SPOTTING SCOPE TO VIEW NESTING STILTS AT AN APPROPRIATE DISTANCE.* Camping, other facilities available at T.O. Fuller State Park.

Directions: *From the intersection of Interstate 55 and Interstate 240 loop in southwest Memphis, take Interstate 55 north to exit 7, US 61 South (Third St.). Travel south on US 61 and turn right (west) on Mitchell Road. Continue 3.6 miles and bear left onto Plant Road. Proceed two miles to the parking lot of T. E. Maxson Wastewater Treatment Facility. Enter white building marked 2685 for information.*

Ownership: City of Memphis (901) 789-0510
Size: 4,500 acres **Closest Town:** Memphis

Since 1981, a small but growing population of gangly black-necked stilts has resided and nested at the EARTH Complex in Memphis. If nests are approached too closely, stilts fly low over the intruder making a loud alarm call, with long red legs trailing.
BARBARA GERLACH

Description: WOA. This site features a mosaic of diverse habitats in close proximity, drawing waterfowl, wild turkeys, Acadian flycatchers, summer and scarlet tanagers, pine warblers, pileated and downy woodpeckers, and slimy and mole salamanders. Many insect species and profuse wildflowers, including azaleas and dwarf iris. Travel the boardwalk for best viewing of white-tailed deer, watersnakes, and prothonotary warblers.

Viewing Information: View from over fifteen miles of trails, and around Big Hill Pond. Boardwalk nearly one mile long passes through Dismal Swamp, offering extensive viewing opportunities and a chance to learn about the wildlife of forested wetlands without getting wet feet. High probability of seeing white-tailed deer and raccoon year-round; also waterfowl, including mallards, gadwall, and American wigeon in winter, and migratory northern waterthrushes and Swainson's thrushes in April, May, and September. Occasional glimpses of wary mink and coyote. A tall tower on Tuscumbia Trail overlooks the Tuscumbia River and Cypress Creek bottoms, with views of soaring birds of prey year-round, and canopy-dwelling nesting birds and squirrels spring and summer. *DEER HUNTING PERMITTED IN SEASON DURING FALL; CHECK WITH PARK OFFICE FOR INFORMATION ON DATES AND SAFETY ZONES.*

Directions: *From Selmer, follow US 45 south seven miles to Eastview. Take TN 57 west ten miles to park entrance. From Memphis, travel west on TN 57 seventy miles to park entrance.*

Ownership: TDEC/BPR (901) 645-7967
Size: 5,023 acres   **Closest Town:** Selmer

The raccoon, Tennessee's state animal, ranges widely across the state but is most common along wooded streams. Raccoons are known for their habit of moistening food, then kneading and tearing it with nimble fingers before eating.

STATE OF TENNESSEE: TOURIST DEVELOPMENT

14 TENNESSEE NATIONAL WILDLIFE REFUGE: BUSSELTOWN UNIT

Description: The smallest and southernmost unit of the Tennessee National Wildlife Refuge includes bottomlands of the Cub Creek Embayment and adjacent Kentucky Lake. Large scale "moist soil management" in the mid-South was pioneered here. This method of raising abundant native wetland food plants produces feeding and resting habitat for wintering waterfowl, and benefits shorebirds, songbirds, and mammals as well.

Viewing Information: Watch for the least sandpiper, dunlin, black-bellied plover, and other shorebirds in migration in early fall and spring, when water levels are low. Bald eagles visit occasionally in winter, also the best time for viewing concentrations of waterfowl. Use auto as a blind to see otter, beaver, occasional rails and other marsh birds in spring. Other viewing opportunities from system roads, from boat, or from Lady Finger Bluff (see site 15). Maps, checklists, and brochures are available at kiosk, or at refuge office in Paris. Some guided tours on request. *OPEN DAYLIGHT HOURS ONLY. INQUIRE ABOUT SEASONAL CLOSURES TO PROTECT WINTERING WATERFOWL. HUNTING PERMITTED FOR SHORT PERIOD IN FALL; INQUIRE FOR DETAILS.*

Directions: *From Parsons, travel two miles east on TN 100 to national wildlife refuge sign. Turn left, following signs approximately six miles to entrance.*

Ownership: USFWS (901) 642-2091
Size: 3,800 acres   **Closest Town:** Parsons

The Tennessee National Wildlife Refuge uses both conventional agricultural farming methods and water level regulation to encourage natural wetland food growth, providing nourishment for over 200,000 ducks and geese each winter.
SCOTT NIELSEN

15 LADY FINGER BLUFF TVA SMALL WILD AREA

Description: Overlooking the former "Narrows" of the Tennessee River, Lady Finger Bluff offers panoramic views and a unique combination of natural features, including wind-gnarled cedars, ancient marine fossils, and limestone sinkholes and springs. Hike through the rich hardwood forest in spring when wild geraniums, jack-in-the-pulpit, and shooting stars bloom. Watch for cottontail rabbits and fence lizards on drier rugged bluffs, and for commercial freshwater mussel fishing in the river below. In autumn and winter, the view from the bluff includes thousands of ducks and geese en route to the Tennessee National Wildlife Refuge (Site 14) on opposite side of river.

Viewing Information: A 2.7-mile round-trip walking trail skirts private coves of Kentucky Lake, passing through hardwood forest up to the high bluff; reverse direction to return. Abundant songbirds along trail in summer. High probability of viewing waterfowl like Canada geese and mallards in flight fall and winter; binoculars are strongly recommended. Watch for green-backed heron at the small pond near trailhead. Fossils of marine animals called crinoids are visible in limestone rock. Contact TVA for free informational brochure. Nearby Mousetail Landing State Park offers camping, picnicking, hiking.

Directions: *From intersection of US 412/TN 100 and TN 13 in Linden, travel 1.8 miles west on US 412/TN 100. Turn right onto paved county road and travel 5.7 miles. Turn east on TN 50, travel 0.8 miles. At this point TN 50 turns sharply; continue straight on paved, then gravel road for total of 4.2 miles. Proceed left on gravel road for 0.1 miles, then left again for 0.7 miles to marked trailhead.*

Ownership: TVA (800) TVA-LAND
Size: Seventy-two acres   **Closest Town:** Linden

A rapid scurrying sound coming from a dry, sunny spot most often reveals the presence of a fence lizard. These spiny, arboreal lizards quickly blend with their surroundings and seemingly disappear, only to reappear doing "push-ups"—a display that reveals the male's blue belly patch and may serve to attract a mate.

HENRY H. HOLDSWORTH

16 NATCHEZ TRACE STATE PARK, STATE FOREST, WMA

Description: Thriving stands of hardwoods and pine have replaced the barren, gullied landscape found here earlier in the century. These forests now teem with gray and fox squirrels, white-tailed deer, raccoons, and wild turkeys. Migrants include the yellow-breasted chat and great crested flycatcher. Watch for the state-listed six-lined racerunner, as well as the copperhead, garter, and hog-nosed snake. Clay crayfish "chimneys" visible along shores of four lakes.

Viewing Information: High probability of viewing deer on TN 114 in early mornings. Visitor center has maps, information, hunting dates and locations. Miles of roads, trails, bridle paths. Site also features Tennessee's largest pecan tree. Observe many acres covered by the invasive Asian kudzu vine along the Fairview Gullies Trail. *USE CAUTION DURING HUNTING SEASONS.*

Directions: *From Interstate 40 east of Jacksonville, take exit 116. Travel south on TN 114 for two miles to Park Visitor Center.*

Ownership: TDEC/BPR (901) 968-3742; TDF (901) 968-6676;
TWRA (901) 423-5725; (800) 372-3928
Size: 48,000 acres   **Closest Town:** Lexington

17 SAM NICKEY WILDLIFE AREA

Description: The tall loblolly pines of the Sam Nickey Wildlife Area are a pleasant contrast to the more common hardwood forests of the Western Plains. Scattered white oaks and sumacs, plus strips of seed-bearing plants, provide wildlife food. Look for pine warblers and golden-crowned kinglets in winter. Prairie warblers and common yellowthroats may be seen in young pines in June. Year-round, watch for gray fox, fox squirrel, red-tailed hawk, or a family of wood ducks on the small ponds in the pine grove.

Viewing Information: Drive slowly or walk through this short gravel spur for moderate probability of viewing white-tailed deer, wild turkey, bobwhite quail, and cottontail rabbit.

Directions: *From TN 69A in Big Sandy, turn left onto Main Street and then immediately right onto Front Street. Turn left at sign to Tennessee National Wildlife Refuge (Site 18), then bear right on Lick Creek Road. Travel 0.9 miles to New Hope Road. Turn left (north) and travel 5.2 miles. At fork in road, bear right on Valentine Branch Road for 0.8 miles. Turn right on forest road into Wildlife Area.*

Ownership: PVT: Westvaco Corporation (901) 642-6500
Size: Sixty-five acres   **Closest Town:** Big Sandy

EXOTIC WILDLIFE IN TENNESSEE: TROUBLE AT HOME

STARLING

ZEBRA MUSSEL

KUDZU

WILD BOAR

The word "exotic" can mean "exciting and different." But in nature, exotic means trouble. Exotics are plants or animals that live in Tennessee natural areas but are native to other continents. They simply don't belong here.

The **European starling** evicts native bluebirds, martins, and flickers from their tree cavity homes. Asian **zebra mussels** encrust boat hulls, clog water intakes, and even attach themselves to native mussels. **Kudzu,** an Asian vine, kills native plants by growing over them—see the effects of kudzu at site 16 in this guide. **Wild boar,** descendants of domestic pigs and the European boar, consume massive amounts of acorns needed by native wildlife. Find out about exotics in your area and learn how you can help prevent further damage.

18 TENNESSEE NATIONAL WILDLIFE REFUGE: BIG SANDY UNIT

Description: WOA. Jutting northward into the confluence of the Big Sandy and Tennessee rivers, Pace Point peninsula is among the best spots for wildlife observation on this northernmost unit of this national wildlife refuge. From late July to mid-September, low water levels leave mudflats exposed during the height of shorebird and tern migration. At this time, probability is high for viewing seven sandpiper species, including the spotted, Baird's, and pectoral; five species of tern, such as the Caspian and Forster's; and rarities, including the white pelican, American avocet, and piping plover. Explore Pace Point and Britton's Ford for twenty-six species of waterfowl—canvasback, lesser scaup, and buffleheads may be seen November to March.

Viewing Information: Viewing from system roads, boat, or along Chickasaw Nature Trail. Maps, checklists, and brochures available at kiosk or refuge office in Paris. During low water conditions, visitors can wade from Pace Point around islands to north, watching for wading birds and shorebirds. *ROAD CONDITIONS MAY BE MUDDY FOLLOWING HEAVY RAINS. OPEN DAYLIGHT HOURS ONLY. INQUIRE ABOUT SEASONAL CLOSURES TO PROTECT WINTERING WATERFOWL. HUNTING PERMITTED FOR SHORT PERIODS IN FALL AND SPRING; INQUIRE ABOUT SAFETY GUIDELINES.*

Directions: *From Paris, take TN 69A to Big Sandy. Turn left onto Main Street, then immediately right onto Front Street. Turn left at sign to refuge, then bear right and follow refuge signs approximately twelve miles to entrance on left.*

Ownership: USFWS (901) 642-2091
Size: 24,000 acres   **Closest Town:** Big Sandy, Paris

A ringing "dew dew dew" advertises the presence of this lanky greater yellow-legs as it forages in shallow water. During migration periods, look for these shorebirds with slightly upturned bills in Tennessee's wetland habitats.
BARBARA GERLACH

Tennessee's great egret populations are growing, thanks to the removal of persistent pesticides from the environment and the efforts of the Tennessee Wildlife Resources Agency. Some of the best places to view these waders include Reelfoot Lake, and Cross Creeks and Hatchie National Wildlife Refuges. BILL LEA

33

LIMESTONE HEARTLAND

Tennessee Coneflowers   TONY MYERS

For eons, the slightly acid waters of Middle Tennessee have gently leached away limestone bedrock. These leaching or dissolving actions continue today, and have formed a one hundred mile-long elliptical basin at the geographic center of the state, known as the Central Basin (see map below). Completely encircling the knoblike hills of the Basin is the Highland Rim, rising up to 1,000 feet above sea level. Oak and hickory forests on the Rim, generously mixed with tulip poplar and maple, contrast with the abundant eastern red cedars in the Basin.

In both the Basin and the Rim, rivulets of rainwater trickle underground into unseen passages, or joints, carving solution caves, sinkholes and other "karst" features. The bedrock of the Limestone Heartland is a honeycomb of thousands of caves, home to highly specialized, slowly growing and slowly reproducing fauna. Solution waters carry away calcium carbonate, used by freshwater mussels in the Cumberland and Tennessee Rivers for building their shells. A freshwater mussel fishing industry thrives in these rivers today.

Rapid movement of water down through surface soils results in a dry, nearly arid landscape despite the fifty inches of rain that falls annually. These unique habitats, known as cedar glades, are found mostly in the Central Basin and support over twenty-five

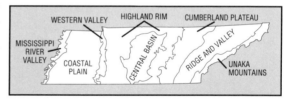

species of rare, drought-adapted plants. Cedar glade habitats may also be the ancestral homes of prairie warblers, field sparrows and other "edge" species still found here today. Common nighthawks, famous denizens of urban areas, were probably abundant here prior to human development, nesting on gravel glades before gravel rooftops existed.

Open lands were likely more abundant here during times of pre-settlement, when prevalent native grasslands supported herds of elk and bison. Land Between The Lakes (site 19) features a herd of bison for viewing today.

Cave Salamander   JACK DERMID

While some of Middle Tennessee's habitats have been altered by urban development and impoundments of the Cumberland and Tennessee Rivers, unique habitats and wildlife viewing opportunities abound. Riverine fish and mussels, as well as species adapted to the deep, dark waters of large reservoirs, are found across the Limestone Heartland.

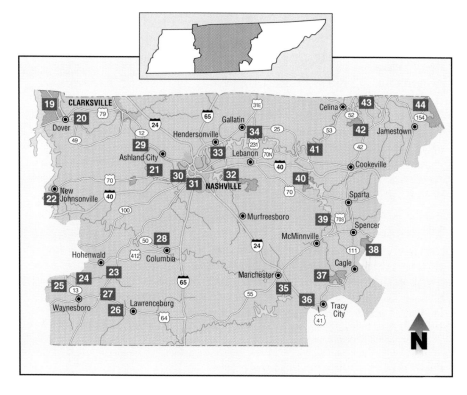

Wildlife Viewing Sites

19 Land Between The Lakes
20 Cross Creeks National Wildlife Refuge
21 Narrows of the Harpeth State Historic Area
22 Tennessee National Wildlife Refuge: Duck River Unit
23 Natchez Trace Parkway
24 Buffalo River
25 Eagle Creek Management Area
26 Granddaddy Branch
27 Laurel Hill Lake
28 Monsanto Ponds Wildlife Observation Area
29 Cheatham Lake
30 Warner Parks
31 Radnor Lake State Natural Area
32 Long Hunter State Park
33 Old Hickory Environmental Study Area
34 Bledsoe Creek State Park
35 Arnold Air Force Base
36 South Cumberland State Recreation Area
37 Savage Gulf State Natural Area
38 Fall Creek Falls State Resort Park
39 Rock Island State Rustic Park
40 Center Hill Dam Overlook
41 Cordell Hull Lake
42 Standing Stone State Park, State Forest and WMA
43 Dale Hollow Lake

19 LAND BETWEEN THE LAKES

Description: Land Between The Lakes, a forty-mile-long peninsula straddling the Tennessee and Cumberland River valleys, is literally the state's heartland. This International Biosphere Reserve supports legendary numbers of white-tailed deer and wild turkey. Over 300 miles of undeveloped shoreline offer ideal habitat for wintering bald eagles, and one of the largest populations of nesting eagles in the mid-South. Other highlights include abundant eastern bluebirds, migratory warblers in spring, and a hummingbird garden. Resident giant Canada geese and introduced fallow deer present year-round.

Viewing Information: Excellent guidebooks, maps, brochures, and checklists available from welcome stations, visitor center, and Woodlands Nature Center. View from over 200 miles hiking trails, horse trails, auto tours. Programs on endangered red wolves and LBL's herd of American bison; many special programs available on request. Annual Eagles Weekends (currently in February) offer popular guided field trips, activities. Seasonal closures of eagle and water-fowl sanctuaries; please observe posted boundaries. *USE CAUTION DURING FALL/SPRING HUNTING SEASONS; AVOID HUNT DATES OR AREAS. ASK STAFF FOR IMPORTANT PRECAUTIONS DURING TICK SEASON.*

Directions: *From Interstate 24, take US 79 thirty-seven miles west through Clarksville, across Cumberland River bridge and through Dover to southern entrance. Turn right, continue north on the Trace for about three miles to south welcome station. Continue north about twenty miles to reach Golden Pond Visitor Center and Planetarium.*

Ownership: TVA (502) 924-5602
Size: 170,000 acres (64,000 in Tennessee)   **Closest Town:** Dover

National symbol on the rebound: bald eagles have recently benefitted from a popular "hacking" program to reintroduce eaglets near large reservoirs. TWRA has led this cooperative program, involving hundreds of volunteers and biologists with federal and state agencies.
KEN L. JENKINS

CROSS CREEKS NATIONAL WILDLIFE REFUGE

Description: WOA. This refuge on the upstream reaches of Lake Barkley provides important resting and feeding habitat for shorebirds spring and fall, and for tens of thousands of waterfowl in winter. Small numbers of endangered bald eagles may be seen year-round. Dabbling ducks visit mid-November through late February. Canada geese abundant; occasional northern shoveler. Diving ducks include redheads, ruddy and ring-necked ducks.

Viewing Information: Over 250 bird species recorded here, from horned larks to wild turkey. High probability of viewing white-tailed deer, gray squirrel, and raccoons year-round. Mississippi Flyway waterfowl easily observed in winter; shorebirds spring and fall. Self-guided auto and walking tours. Staffed visitor center, open weekdays, offers checklists and maps. *CALL FOR DATES, LOCATIONS OF WINTER SANCTUARY CLOSURES. SOME ROADS SUBJECT TO FLOODING.*

Directions: *From junction of US 79 and TN 49 in Dover, travel three miles east on TN 49. Sign to office/visitor center.*

Ownership: USFWS (615) 232-7477
Size: 8,862 acres
Closest Town: Dover

NARROWS OF THE HARPETH STATE HISTORIC AREA

Description: *CANOE VIEWING.* The quality riverine habitat of the free-flowing Harpeth State Scenic River provides excellent birding, especially during migrations. Canoes are good blinds, affording views of muskrats, softshell turtles, water snakes, beaver, belted kingfishers, swallows, and barred and great horned owls. Rich floodplain offers spring displays of showy wildflowers.

Viewing Information: This state-owned property includes launch and takeout sites for canoeing; additional access options also available. Nearby outfitters offer canoe rentals, services. Avoid crowds on warm-season weekends. Class I waters appropriate for beginners. *WEAR LIFE JACKETS AT ALL TIMES. RIVER BANKS ARE PRIVATELY OWNED. CHECK WATER LEVELS TO ENSURE A QUALITY FLOAT TRIP; CALL OFFICE BEFORE MAKING CANOE TRIP.*

Directions: *From Interstate 40 in west Nashville, take US 70 West exit. Travel fourteen miles west on US 70. Turn right (north) onto Cedar Hill Road—turn is east of Harpeth River bridge. Travel 2.7 miles and turn left to reach launch site, historic tunnel and trailhead, bearing left again at 0.2 miles. Or, travel 2.9 miles and turn right to reach takeout.*

Ownership: TDEC/BPR (615) 797-9052
Size: Fifteen acres, seven river miles
Closest Town: Pegram

22 TENNESSEE NATIONAL WILDLIFE REFUGE: DUCK RIVER UNIT

Description: WOA. The confluence of the Duck and Tennessee rivers is the focal viewing area of this site. Tens of thousands of wintering Canada geese, mallards, gadwall, black ducks, American wigeons, and pintails feed on native plants and in fields of winter wheat, millet, and corn. Bald eagles may be seen here year-round; look for occasional golden eagles during winter months. Grassy Lake features a great blue heron rookery, or nesting colony—please view herons from a distance with binoculars or a spotting scope. Herons, as well as oprey, nest in summer. Abundant songbirds include yellow warblers and orchard orioles. During warmer months, watch for thirty-eight species of amphibians and fifty-two varieties of reptiles, including six poisonous snakes. Lower probability of viewing river otter, mink, rails, and bitterns.

Viewing Information: View from refuge roads or from boat. Dikes open to foot travel seasonally. Maps, checklists, and brochures available from kiosk or refuge office in Paris. Some guided tours upon request. *ENTIRE DUCK RIVER BOTTOMS MAY BE IMPASSABLE DURING FLOOD SEASON; CHECK WITH OFFICE FOR ROAD CONDITIONS. OPEN DAYLIGHT HOURS ONLY. HUNTING PERMITTED FOR SHORT PERIODS SPRING AND FALL; INQUIRE FOR DETAILS. INQUIRE ABOUT SEASONAL CLOSURES TO PROTECT WINTERING WATERFOWL AND NESTING HERONS.*

Directions: *From US 70 in New Johnsonville, turn south on Long Street. Travel 2.6 miles to stop, turn left, and proceed 0.3 miles. Turn right, traveling 0.6 miles to refuge entrance on left.*

Ownership: USFWS (901) 642-2091
Size: 25,000 acres
Closest Town: New Johnsonville

Lake and wetland habitats in winter and spring feature the brilliant and ungainly northern shoveler, as well as other "dabbling" ducks. Shovelers strain plankton through the comblike edges of their huge bills.
JOHN GERLACH

Description: Once a series of secretive Indian trails along ridgetops, the Natchez Trace Parkway now stretches as a ribbon of green across Tennessee's Nashville Basin and Highland Rim, and portions of two other states. Observant visitors will encounter white-tailed deer, woodchucks, and box turtles, and the musky scent of skunks. Also watch for coyote, fox, and wild turkey along edges at dawn and dusk. At one of the many stops and pull-outs look for gray squirrels and eastern chipmunks, and such reptiles as fence lizards and skinks. Especially in early morning, note common crows patrolling for carrion.

Viewing Information: Extremely well-maintained and clearly signed, the parkway provides high quality viewing from an automobile. Watch for loggerhead shrikes, eastern bluebirds, and American ketrels perched on power lines over fields. Try milepost 403 or 375 for forested routes of the original Trace. Sweetwater Branch Nature Trail (Mile 363) traverses rich creek bottom habitat and is a good birdwatching stop. Map and brochures available at six Tennessee locations, including Meriwether Lewis (Mile 385) near Hohenwald. Parkway also accesses Laurel Hill Lake (Site 27). Posted speed limit strictly enforced.

Directions: *Current northern (temporary) terminus is thirteen miles southwest of Franklin at TN 46. An additional fourteen miles under construction to TN 100 near Pasquo. Tennessee's southern terminus is Alabama state line near Cypress Inn.*

Ownership: NPS (601) 680-4025
Size: Eighty-eight miles in Tennessee
Closest Town: Leipers Fork, Hohenwald

White-tailed deer quietly appear along roadsides and field edges in late afternoons and early mornings. Their calcium-rich antlers are shed in autumn, and are quickly devoured by mice and other rodents.

BILL LEA

39

24 BUFFALO RIVER

Description: CANOE VIEWING. The emerald green waters of the Buffalo River flow northward across forested and pastoral middle Tennessee, free of impoundment over the entire floatable stretch of 110 miles. Renowned for its aquatic diversity, the river supports over eighty-five species of fish, many visible to floaters, such as smallmouth bass, coppercheek darters, and spotfin chubs. Rounding one of the river's many bends, expect to surprise a green-backed or great blue heron; also present are mammals such as mink and muskrat, and reptiles, including the banded watersnake and several turtle species. Double-crested cormorants, wood ducks, and mallards are especially abundant in winter near the confluence of the Buffalo and Duck rivers.

Viewing Information: Commercial outfitters offer services along river during warmer months. All sections of river suitable for beginning canoeists. Upper portion of river between Henryville and Flatwoods is floatable November through August; remainder of river year-round. Weekday trips during warm season offer greater solitude and optimal wildlife viewing. Lawrence Co. portion is state scenic river. *RIVER BANKS ARE PRIVATE PROPERTY—RESPECT RIGHTS OF LANDOWNERS. WEAR SAFETY FLOTATION AT ALL TIMES.*

Directions: *Access river from Interstate 40 at exit 143, east of Tennessee River. TN 13 south parallels river through Lobelville, Linden, and Flatwoods. Headwaters near Henryville. Nineteen access points available.*

Ownership: PVT; TDEC/SRP (615) 532-0034
Size: 120 river miles
Closest Town: Linden

The Tennessee Scenic Rivers Act of 1968 established the nation's first statewide comprehensive scenic rivers program. The program protects eleven outstanding rivers in Tennessee, including the headwaters of the Buffalo River in Lawrence County. STATE OF TENNESSEE: TOURIST DEVELOPMENT

25 EAGLE CREEK MANAGEMENT AREA

Description: On this extensive tract of industrially-managed timberland, watch for yellow-breasted chats and prairie warblers in the younger forests. Red-tailed hawks, also downy and red-bellied woodpeckers inhabit newly cleared areas. Look for woodcock in moist fields, bobwhite quail along field edges. View white-tailed deer and wild turkey on remote roads.

Viewing Information: Early morning, weekend, and late afternoon visits best for viewing. Contact owner or TWRA for maps and information. Try Buck Trail or Beech Trail; horse trails. *WATCH FOR LOGGING TRUCKS ON MAIN GRAVEL ROADS. CONTACT DISTRICT MANAGER FOR DETAILS ON HUNTING SEASONS. WEAR BLAZE ORANGE DURING HUNTING SEASON.*

Directions: *From intersection of US 64 and TN 13 in Waynesboro, take US 64 west 0.2 miles, turn right (west) onto Clifton Turnpike. Continue for two miles to southeast entrance. To reach main viewing roads, continue four miles and turn left onto Road 1 (C.C. Road), or travel one additional mile and turn right onto Road 17 (Pea Ridge Road).*

Ownership: PVT; Champion International Corporation, (615) 722-3648; managed in cooperation with TWRA (615) 781-6622 or (800) 624-7406
Size: 22,250 acres   **Closest Town:** Waynesboro

26 GRANDDADDY BRANCH

Description: The waters of crystal-clear Granddaddy Branch support a diversity of fish, including darters, while the rich creek bottom forest carpeted with ferns and doll's eyes offers views of scarlet tanagers, and mating damselflies. Watch for wild turkey or raccoon tracks along stream banks.

Viewing Information: Beauty and solitude are the reasons to visit this site. The waterfalls, cool cove, high bluffs, and moist forest of sugar maple, beech, and spicebush are secluded and scenic. Follow the creek downstream along an old road bed, then bear left to reach a one-half-mile trail to New Twin Falls.

Directions: *From intersection of US 64 and US 43 in Lawrenceburg travel west for 10.2 miles on US 64. Turn left (south) onto Hood Road and travel 4.4 miles (becomes gravel after two miles). Turn right and travel 0.3 miles, fording the stream. Continue 0.1 miles and park at entrance to old woods road on right. CREEK MAY FLOOD IN WINTER; DO NOT ATTEMPT TO FORD.*

Ownership: PVT; Champion International Corporation (615) 722-3648
Size: Fifty acres   **Closest Town:** Lawrenceburg

Extensive forests are the preferred home of the pileated woodpecker, easily identified in flight by its flashing white underwings and crowlike size. These birds excavate holes that will eventually become homes for barred owls, wood ducks, kestrels, squirrels, snakes, and other forest creatures. BILL LEA

27 LAUREL HILL LAKE

Description: WOA. Located within the forested 14,000-acre Laurel Hill Wildlife Management Area, this reservoir and its surrounding marshland and thickets offer diverse viewing opportunities. Winter waterfowl include surface feeding or dabbling ducks, including mallards and gadwall; diving ducks such as lesser scaup; and common loons. Beavers and swamp rabbits inhabit wetlands. Many warblers present during migration, including the yellow, magnolia, and bay-breasted. Look for nesting osprey in summer. WMA primarily managed to enhance habitat for bobwhite quail, gray squirrel, cottontail rabbit, mourning dove, white-tailed deer, and turkey. Dispersed viewing from gravel roads.

Viewing Information: Viewing opportunities are concentrated around lake. Probabililty for waterfowl high in winter—look for bufflehead and wood ducks. Potholes and mudflats exposed during winter attract such shorebirds as the common snipe, killdeer, and an occasional American pipit. Dependable year-round viewing of great blue herons, belted kingfishers, giant Canada geese, and eastern bluebirds. Maps available at office on-site. *CHECK HUNTING DATES BEFORE VISITING WILDLIFE MANAGEMENT AREA.*

Directions: *From the junction of US 43 and US 64 in Lawrenceburg, travel west 14.5 miles on US 64. Turn right onto Brush Creek Road and travel two miles to lake. Additional access from Natchez Trace Parkway, three miles north of junction with US 64: turn right on Brush Creek Road, proceed 1.5 miles, turn left to lake.*

Ownership: TWRA (615) 762-7200 or (615) 781-6622; (800) 624-7406
Size: 327-acre reservoir; 14,000-acre WMA   **Closest Town:** Lawrenceburg

Industrious to some, ornery to others, the beaver is capable of felling a three-inch diameter tree in ten minutes. Common in wetlands throughout Tennessee, they are most often detected by the sound of their warning tail slap on the water, and may be seen near their dams, lodges and gnaw marks.
LEONARD LEE RUE III

28 | MONSANTO PONDS WILDLIFE OBSERVATION AREA

Description: WOA. These extensive marshlands surrounding former settling ponds have created a premier birding destination. A 200-acre portion of Monsanto's 5,000-acre holding is a state-designated Wildlife Observation Area. At least 160 species of birds have been sighted here, including the least bittern, sora, common moorhen, and Virginia rail—look for these species fall and spring. Other wading birds such as the green-backed, great blue, and black-crowned night heron are readily observed in warmer months. Uncommon willow flycatchers and warbling vireos appear in summer. Winter brings ring-necked ducks, mallards, lesser scaup, pintails, and an occasional ruddy duck.

Viewing Information: This award-winning site adjacent to the Duck River features a visitor kiosk with maps and brochures and unique public use blinds, including one barrier-free blind. Binoculars and spotting scopes strongly suggested for best views of waterfowl, marsh birds, and songbirds.

Directions: *From downtown Columbia, travel approximately four miles west on TN 50. Turn right on Monsanto Road and travel about three miles to the visitor kiosk at the eastern end of area.*

Ownership: PVT; Monsanto Company (615) 380-9333
Size: 200 acres public access; 5,000 acres wildlife habitat enhancement area
Closest Town: Columbia

The Monsanto Company, in cooperation with TWRA, has developed a wildlife management plan to maintain freshwater marsh habitat at a former phosphate mining plant. This site is an outstanding example of private industry efforts towards conservation. MONSANTO COMPANY

Description: WOA. Cheatham Lake is a vital waterfowl stopover and wintering area. Many ducks, including mallards, black ducks, pintails, northern shovelers, and gadwall are all likely visitors during colder months. Scan the winter fields for swamp sparrows, horned larks, and American pipits. Warbler migration peaks in early May and late September. In summer, watch for yellow-crowned night herons, also occasional mink, muskrat, beaver, and watersnakes. Shorebird viewing best during early fall migration. Hundreds of gregarious cliff swallows tend their jug-shaped nests attached to Cheatham Dam May through July. Adjacent pine forest attracts brown creepers, ruby-crowned and golden-crowned kinglets, and occasional long-eared owls in winter.

Viewing Information: Viewing from three areas along Cheatham Lake—Dyson Ditch, Hudgen's Slough, and Cheatham Lock & Dam. The first two areas offer similar opportunities for waterfowl, songbirds, and freshwater mammals. *AVOID DYSON DITCH AND HUDGEN'S SLOUGH DURING HUNTING SEASONS SEPTEMBER-JANUARY. DYSON DITCH REFUGE CLOSED TO PUBLIC ACCESS OCTBER 15 - FEBRUARY 1.* Cheatham Lock and Dam offers views of cliff swallows. Park at lock and dam, walk across lock on metal catwalk: swallow nests, are attached to upper part of dam. Use binoculars for optimal viewing of nesting activities. Parking and hiking at all sites; damsite offers restrooms, picnicing, boat launching, and camping April-October.

Directions: *From junction of TN 12 and TN 49 in Ashland City:* **Hudgen's Slough**—*travel southwest on TN 49 for 2.4 miles. Turn right into Bluff Creek Launching Ramp site. Walk or drive primitive roads along reservoir, wet fields.* **Dyson Ditch**—*travel north on TN 12 for 1.1 miles. Turn left onto Chapmansboro Road at Sycamore Creek Recreation Area sign. Continue straight and cross bridge, then stay right on Chapmansboro for total 4.6 miles. Turn left into undeveloped parking area at Cheatham Reservoir WMA sign. Walk or drive primitive roads.* **Cheatham Dam**—*travel 7.4 miles north on TN 12. Left on Cheatham Dam Road, travel 4.5 miles to lock and dam.*

Ownership: USACOE (615) 254-3734; leased to TWRA (615) 792-4510 or (800) 624-7406
Size: 1,250 acres (5,152 acres WMA)
Closest Town: Ashland City

Snakes have spines that contain up to 400 vertebrae, each connected to a pair of protective ribs. Human spines, by comparison, have only 33 vertebrae.

30 WARNER PARKS

Description: Geologic forces have worn limestones into a series of rugged knobs and rolling uplands. The Warner Parks, one of Tennessee's largest urban parks, have become an island of nature in a sea of development. Moist forests on northern and lower slopes, drier conditions atop the knobs and on south and west-facing slopes, modest ribbons of creek bottoms. Birds and wildflowers are the most dependable offerings, including hairy woodpeckers, cerulean warblers, and barred owls. A study of eastern bluebirds has continued since 1930s. Small mammals are frequently seen; raccoons, opossums, foxes, coyotes, and white-tailed deer are also present and more difficult to see.

Viewing Information: Spectacular haven for solitude in highly urban setting. Extensive system of paved roads, bridle paths, eleven miles of foot trails. Extensive public and group programming through nature center. Observations of wildlife likely, high quality, at all seasons; large concentrations of wildlife not likely. Impressive and diverse plant communities feature grand old beeches, oaks, black walnuts, and tulip poplars. Many demonstration projects of citizen involvement, including exotic plant control, occur through active Friends group.

Directions: *From Interstate 65 south of Nashville, take Old Hickory Boulevard exit in Brentwood. Proceed west approximately eight miles on Old Hickory. At junction with TN 100 turn left (south) and proceed to Nature Center entrance.*

Ownership: Metropolitan Board of Parks and Recreation-Nashville, Warner Park Nature Center (615) 352-6299
Size: 2,665 acres
Closest Town: Nashville

The Tennessee Department of Environment and Conservation, Friends of Warner Parks, and Tennessee Division of Forestry have initiated a long-term inventory of the park's plant communities. The study will monitor the spread of unwanted introduced plants and provide direction to restore natural integrity, where needed, to park habitats.
STATE OF TENNESSEE: TOURIST DEVELOPMENT

31 RADNOR LAKE STATE NATURAL AREA

Description: WOA. High limestone knobs surround the impounded valley of Otter Creek in suburban Nashville, where citizen activism led to the establishment of Radnor Lake as Tennessee's first and most visited state natural area. The forested slopes of this watershed escaped development–maturing tulip poplars, maples, and beech trees shelter April wildflowers. Exceptional birding during spring and fall migrations; nesting prothonotary warblers and Louisiana waterthrushes are summer highlights. Patient observers will encounter fox, beaver, opossum, white-tailed deer, and occasional coyote and bobcat. Shallow waters harbor green-backed herons and many turtle species, including slider and softshell, seen basking year-round. Winter brings over twenty-three species of waterfowl, including lesser scaup, pied-billed grebe, and bufflehead. Wood ducks nest in sheltered coves; ducklings commonly appear in May.

Viewing Information: Extensive trail system accessed from two parking areas. During heavy visitation, Otter Creek Road closes to vehicles and becomes a paved walkway for observation. Numerous guided tours, programs, and demonstrations scheduled primarily spring and fall; on request other seasons. Weekday visits recommended for optimal viewing.

Directions: In Nashville, take exit 78A from Interstate 65. Travel west on Harding Place 0.6 miles to Franklin Road (US 31). Turn left (south) onto Franklin Road and travel 1.5 miles. Turn right (west) onto Otter Creek Road and continue 2.6 miles to visitor center. Otter Creek Road bisects the area.

Ownership: TDEC/BPR (615) 373-3467
Size: 1,025 acres   **Closest Town:** Nashville

Only during fall and spring migration do Nashville warblers visit their namesake city, Tennessee's state capital. This bird was first discovered by biologist Alexander Wilson nearly 200 years ago, and he named it for his location at the time.

JOHN GERLACH

A HONEYCOMB OF STONE: THE KARST TERRAIN

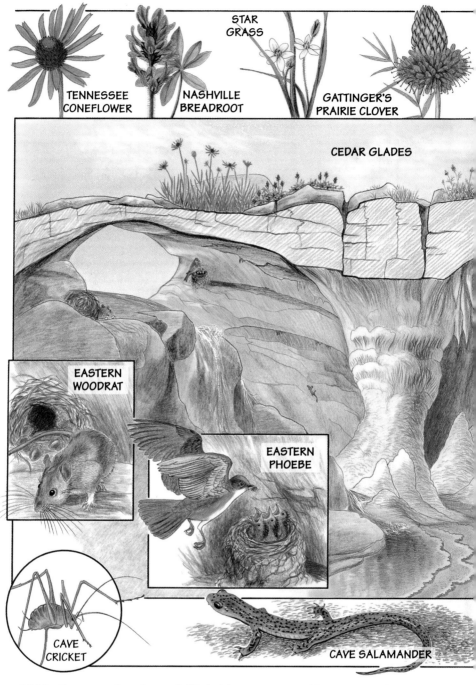

STAR GRASS

TENNESSEE CONEFLOWER

NASHVILLE BREADROOT

GATTINGER'S PRAIRIE CLOVER

CEDAR GLADES

EASTERN WOODRAT

EASTERN PHOEBE

CAVE CRICKET

CAVE SALAMANDER

Middle Tennessee's unique wildlife habitats are created by patterns of water movement. Rainfall percolates through cracks in limestone bedrock, creating arid, prairie-like cedar glades on the surface, home to many rare and colorful plants.

Surface streams disappear and re-emerge as springs in "karst" or limestone terrain. Underground water dissolves bedrock to form caves, where three distinct wildlife habitats are found. Phoebes nest in crevices near the **cave entrance.**

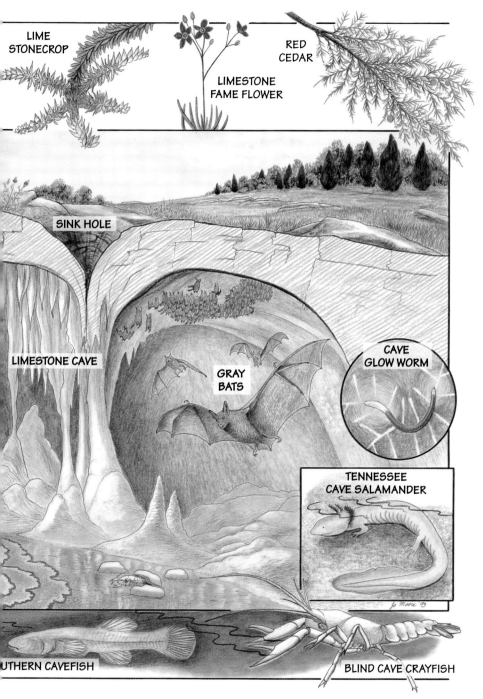

LIME
STONECROP

LIMESTONE
FAME FLOWER

RED
CEDAR

SINK HOLE

LIMESTONE CAVE

GRAY
BATS

CAVE
GLOW WORM

TENNESSEE
CAVE SALAMANDER

UTHERN CAVEFISH

BLIND CAVE CRAYFISH

Jo Moore '93

Cave crickets, eastern woodrats, and raccoons move in and out of the **twilight zone,** where their droppings form the base of a food web. Pale eyeless fish and crayfish live in the **dark zone,** where bats may spend all or part of their lives, hibernating or raising young.

Tennessee's limestone-sandstone habitats may be seen at sites 32, 44, and 57 in this guide. These rare ecosystems are extremely fragile—please treat them with care.

32 LONG HUNTER STATE PARK

Description: This state park stretches along thirty miles of the eastern shoreline of 14,000-acre J. Percy Priest Lake. On this narrow strip of limestone bluff land lies the full complement of original Middle Tennessee habitats, including dry hardwood forests, red cedar forests, cedar glades, and prairie land. Watch for such birds as green-backed, great blue and yellow-crowned night herons, loons, and wintering waterfowl. Other attractions include a population of pure white (gray) squirrels along the two-mile, barrier-free trail encircling 140-acre Couchville Lake. Moderate to low probability of viewing osprey on the lake during warmer months. White-tailed deer may be seen year-round.

Viewing Information: Outstanding trails and visitor center interpret the flora and fauna of Middle Tennessee's unique cedar glades. Twenty species of waterfowl may be seen on J. Percy Priest Lake in winter. Incredible cedar glade flora is a must for summer visitors. Small mammals and six-lined racerunners abundant. Look for uncommon glade-adapted land snails. Abundant killdeer, common nighthawk, and prairie warbler. *AVOID SPRING, EARLY SUMMER CROWDS BY VISITING ON WEEKDAYS. PLEASE HELP PROTECT THESE UNIQUE PLANT COMMUNITIES—DO NOT REMOVE OR DISTURB PLANTS.*

Directions: *From Interstate 40 east of Nashville, take exit 226A (Mt. Juliet) and travel 6.7 miles south on TN 171. Turn left into park entrance. Visitor center on immediate right. Or, from Interstate 24 south of Nashville, take exit 62 (Old Hickory Boulevard). Travel seven miles north on TN 171. Turn right into park entrance. Park has numerous access points; inquire about additional directions.*

Ownership: TDEC/BPR (615) 885-2422
Size: 2,400 acres   **Closest Town:** Mount Juliet

The limestone fameflower, a rare, diminutive plant of Tennessee's cedar glades, blooms only for a few hours each afternoon. Once considered barren wastelands, cedar glades are now reknowned for their beauty and scientific importance.
TONY MYERS

33 OLD HICKORY ENVIRONMENTAL STUDY AREA

Description: WOA. Along the shores of Old Hickory Lake, this educational site offers ideas for backyard wildlife plantings—sumacs and hackberry for songbirds, black walnut and osage orange for squirrels, and milkweeds for butterflies. The open fields support goldfinches, eastern bluebirds, bobwhite quail, and eastern cottontail rabbits. Giant Canada geese are year-round residents. Protected cove and sloughs draw common loon, horned and pied-billed grebe, and mallard ducks in winter. Year-round, look for green-backed and yellow-crowned night heron. Beaver activity and lodging evident along shoreline.

Viewing Information: Popular site with residents and school groups. Informal trails lead viewers among wildlife plantings and around fields to lake. Use binoculars for optimal viewing of waterfowl, herons, songbirds.

Directions: *From Nashville, travel north on Interstate 65 ten miles. Take exit 95 (TN 386/Vietnam Veterans Boulevard). Travel 2.7 miles; take TN 31E north towards Hendersonville (becomes Gallatin Road). Travel 2.2 miles, and turn right on Walton Ferry Road. Travel 1.6 miles to gravel parking area on right.*

Ownership: USACOE (615) 822-4846
Size: Twenty-five acres   **Closest Town:** Hendersonville

34 BLEDSOE CREEK STATE PARK

Description: WOA. A variety of habitats in close proximity offer diverse viewing. Look for waterfowl in winter, including Canada geese and mallards. Great blue and black-crowned night herons are common, particularly in summer and fall. Songbirds include the eastern bluebird, eastern meadowlark, blue grosbeak, field and chipping sparrow, and occasional loggerhead shrike. Barred and great-horned owls present year-round. Migrant songbirds spring and fall.

Viewing Information: Try the High Ridge Trail for spring wildflowers. Birdsong and Shoreline Trails offer views of shorebirds in fall migration, songbirds year-round, also fish, snapping turtles and sliders. High probability of viewing white-tailed deer fall and winter. Park accomodates RV campers. Check with park office for brochures, details on seasonal programs.

Directions: *From Interstate 40 in Lebanon, take exit 238. Travel north twenty-two miles on US 231 to TN 25. Turn left (west) onto TN 25 and proceed eight miles to Zieglers Fort Road. Turn left (south) and travel 1.4 miles. Left into entrance.*

Ownership: TDEC/BPR (615) 452-3706
Size: 165 acres   **Closest Town:** Gallatin

35 ARNOLD AIR FORCE BASE

Description: This wildlife management area features prairie-like "barrens," wetland hardwood forests, and stands of pine. Songbirds seen here include the prairie warbler, blue grosbeak, acadian flycatcher, eastern kingbird, and grasshopper sparrow. Woods Reservoir on the south end of the base attracts waterfowl, including mallards, redheads, lesser scaup, gadwall, and coots in winter. Endangered gray bats roost on Woods Reservoir Dam mid-May through September; at dusk, watch them feed on insects from south shore below dam.

Viewing Information: Contact USAF or TWRA for maps and information before visiting. High probability of viewing white-tailed deer on roadsides year-round. Waterfowl may be seen at Woods Reservoir November through March. Peak viewing of migratory birds May through July. Nesting great blue herons at Sinking Pond. Terrestrial orchids and dwarf iris bloom spring and summer; showy sunflowers in fall. Tennessee Native Plant Society occasionally offers guided tours. *VIEWING NOT ALLOWED DURING BIG GAME SEASON, TYPICALLY SATURDAYS AND SUNDAYS SEPTEMBER-DECEMBER.*

Directions: *To reach Sinking Pond, take exit 117 from Interstate 24. Travel 0.3 miles south on Wattendorf Memorial Highway, turning right on Hillsboro Road. Travel 2.3 miles paved, additional 2.3 miles gravel road to small pull-off on left. Cross road on foot and follow an old road bed to swamp forest. To reach Woods Dam, travel about three miles west on TN 279 from its junction with TN 127. Turn right on paved road to Elk River Dam; road ends in gravel loop below dam.*

Ownership: USAF (615) 454-4066; managed in cooperation with TWRA (615) 967-6101 or (800) 624-7406
Size: 39,081 acres
Closest Town: Tullahoma, Manchester

The Tennessee Native Plant Society, based at the University of Tennessee-Knoxville's Botany Department, invites the public to join the group in viewing, photographing and conserving the state's native flora.

LAURA MITCHELL

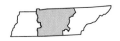

36 SOUTH CUMBERLAND STATE RECREATION AREA

Description: The upland hardwood forests of this Cumberland Plateau site surround scenic waterfalls, caves, sandstone formations, and limestone sinks, interlaced with a freshwater marsh, small pond, and old fields. Birding best in migration and summer; watch for worm-eating and black-and-white warblers, rose-breasted grosbeaks, and scarlet tanagers; eastern bluebirds are seen year-round. Game species include white-tailed deer, cottontail rabbits, ruffed grouse, and bobwhite quail. Amphibians here include American toads and the blind Tennessee cave salamander. Visit wetlands in late summer for wildflowers.

Viewing Information: The South Cumberland Visitor Center is information hub for all units in the South Cumberland State Recreation Area complex, including Fiery Gizzard Trail, Carter Caves State Natural Area, Grundy Forest State Natural Area, Grundy Lakes State Park, Savage Gulf State Natural Area, and TVA's Foster Falls Small Wild Area. Some guided tours offered through visitor center. Extensive trail system, including Meadow Trail with loops of variable length, and Fiery Gizzard Trail with spectacular vistas, vultures and broad-winged hawks. *THE ROCKY TERRAIN SUPPORTS ABUNDANT COPPERHEADS AND TIMBER RATTLESNAKES—OBSERVE THESE POISON-OUS SNAKES FROM A SAFE DISTANCE. USE CAUTION DURING HUNTING SEASON LATE NOVEMBER-DECEMBER. RESPECT RIGHTS OF ALL PRIVATE LANDOWNERS ALONG TRAILS. USE CAUTION AT OVERLOOKS AND WATERFALLS.*

Directions: *In Monteagle, take exit 134 from Interstate 24. Follow signs three miles south on US 41 to South Cumberland Visitor Center on left.*

Ownership: TDEC/BPR (615) 924-2980 or (615) 924-2956; PVT
Size: 841 acres   **Closest Town:** Monteagle

Higher elevation forests in the Cumberlands and eastern mountains are summer homes to the rose-breasted grosbeak. These birds are found in migration throughout the state, and can be identified by sharp call notes ("eek"), melodious song, and a strong conical bill used for cracking seeds and berries.

A. MORRIS/VIREO

37 SAVAGE GULF STATE NATURAL AREA

Description: At Savage Gulf, the level Cumberland Plateau crumbles into rugged gorges or "gulfs" 1,000 feet deep, cut by creeks that tumble to valleys below. Three gulfs, including the exquisite old growth forests of Savage Gulf, comprise this beautiful area for wildlife viewing and solitude. Some wildlife highlights include white-tailed deer, five woodpecker species, ruby-throated hummingbirds, smoky and masked shrews, and migratory birds such as the black-throated green warbler and golden-crowned kinglet. Several varieties of land snail may be seen, as well as wildflowers including turtleheads and Wood's false hellebore. Also fall-blooming gentians, and ferns in small riparian wetlands atop plateau. Tall hemlocks and umbrella trees throughout gorges.

Viewing Information: Access from Great Stone Door (barrier-free) or Savage Gulf entrances. View from over fifty miles of trails and overlooks. High probability of seeing white-tailed deer, also downy and pileated woodpeckers year-round. Trail overlooks feature eye-level views of soaring red-shouldered hawks and turkey vultures. Songbirds are present in modest numbers year-round, including migratory visitors like the gray-cheeked thrush and Nashville warbler. Visitor Center near Monteagle (open seven days) offers maps, trail information, and interpretive displays. Public access to old growth forest prohibited except during guided tours. *USE CAUTION DURING LATE NOVEMBER-DECEMBER WEEKEND HUNTING SEASONS, AND WHEN VISITING OVER-LOOKS AND WATERFALLS.*

*Directions: In Monteagle, take exit 134 from Interstate 24. Follow signs three miles south on US 41 to South Cumberland Visitor Center on left. Continue three miles and turn left (north) on TN 56 at signal in Tracy City. **Stone Door Entrance:** Continue north on TN 56 for fifteen miles to Beersheba Springs. Right at Park sign, follow signs for two miles to ranger station. **Savage Gulf Entrance:** Continue north on TN 56 and turn right (east) onto TN 108. Drive ten miles and turn left (north) onto TN 399. Drive five miles to Savage Gulf entrance sign,left to ranger station.*

Ownership: TDEC/BPR (615) 924-2980, (615) 924-2956
Size: 11,500 acres
Closest Town: Palmer (Savage Gulf), Beersheba Springs (Stone Door)

The American chestnut was once an abundant tree in Tennessee's forests, supplying nutritious nuts for birds and mammals. A fungal disease called chestnut blight, introduced from Asia, resulted in the loss of this tree by the 1940s.

Description: Misty gorges of towering tulip populars and hemlocks, and the tallest waterfall east of the Rocky Mountains await visitors to this scenic site. The park features unique sandstone "rockhouse" habitats, home to eastern woodrats, eastern phoebes, and orb weavers, spiders known for their beautiful webs. White-breasted nuthatches are common; check hemlocks for black-throated green warblers and occasional blackburnian warblers in summer. White-tailed deer, eastern chipmunks, and box turtles are common; wild turkeys, wood ducks, and cave salamanders are uncommon; bobcats rare. More than 216 plant species; 118 bird species present.

Viewing Information: Many miles of roads and trails. Explore trails along rim of Cane Creek Gorge for eye-level views of soaring turkey vultures. Lakeside Trail also productive. White-tailed deer and ruffed grouse may be seen year-round. Songbirds best seen spring and summer; look for wood thrush, oven-bird, and scarlet and summer tanagers. Hikers often see woodchuck and gray squirrel, American and Fowler's toads, eastern newt, and the hognose, garter or black rat snakes. Gray fox, striped skunk, and copperhead snake are also present. Visitor Center and Inn offer maps, brochures, trail guides, field guides. *USE CAUTION ON OVERLOOKS AND WATERFALLS. OBSERVE POISONOUS SNAKES FROM A DISTANCE.*

Directions: Northern Entrance: *From intersection of US 127 and TN 30 in Pikeville, turn west on TN 30 and travel to junction with TN 284. Proceed south.* **Southern Entrance:** *From intersection of TN 30 and TN 111 in Spencer, turn south on TN 111. Travel to junction of TN 284. Proceed east.*

Ownership: TDEC/BPR (615) 881-5708
Size: 16,030 acres   **Closest Town:** Pikeville

Erosion-resistant sandstone capping the Cumberland Plateau has formed prominent cliffs and spectacular waterfalls. Some plants and animals are specially adapted to the "spray zone" at the base of Fall Creek Falls, under the shadow of water plunging 256 feet into a shaded gorge.

STATE OF TENNESSEE: TOURIST DEVELOPMENT

39 ROCK ISLAND STATE RUSTIC PARK

Description: The waters of the Caney Fork River gorge attract flying insects, which in turn draw bats, including the big brown bat and pipistrelle—they are readily seen from the Great Falls platform in summer, feeding at dusk. Rock Island also features one of the largest concentrations of black vultures in the state; the birds roost adjacent to the swimming area on Center Hill Lake. Protected coves offer spectacular spring wildflowers.

Viewing Information: Observation platform and trail to gorge are accessible from Great Falls picnic area. Yellow-crowned night herons are common in gorge in summer. Try the peninsula trail, accessed from power generating station, for a variety of butterflies. Watch for wild turkey along the Collins Nature Trail. White-tailed deer are common. Occasional guided pontoon tours offered to summer campers only.

Directions: From junction of TN 56 and US 70S in McMinnville, travel east thirteen miles on US 70S. Turn left (south) onto TN 287, and follow signs to park office.

Ownership: TDEC/BPR (615) 686-2471
Size: 883 acres   **Closest Town:** McMinnville

40 CENTER HILL DAM OVERLOOK

Description: This site features panoramic views and, in the early morning, congregations of turkey and black vultures, and rough-winged and barn swallows below the dam. Occasional wintering eagles in large trees below dam; many winter gulls of two species. Listen for loons around dusk, fall and winter.

Viewing Information: Barrier-free access at dam site. Check open areas around lake for eastern bluebirds, eastern meadowlarks, and common flicker. Large numbers of white-tailed deer and raccoon may be viewed dusk and dawn on secluded, forested roads, and in meadows along the lake and river. Best viewing on weekdays during warm season. Adjacent 6,000-acre Edgar Evins State Park offers services and eye-level views of songbirds in the treetops year-round from tower.

Directions: From Interstate 40 west of Cookeville, take exit 268 (Buffalo Valley). Travel three miles south on TN 96. Turn right on TN 141 and travel one-half mile to dam overlook.

Ownership: USACOE (615) 858-3125; TDEC/BPR (615) 858-2446
Size: Fifty acres   **Closest Town:** Cookeville

The wild turkey is known for its wary nature—except during mating season, when any loud noise, including the slam of a car door or a clap of thunder, can incite tom turkeys to gobble. Vigorous conservation efforts of the TWRA have resulted in impressive population growth, making turkeys more accessible to wildlife viewers.
JOHN GERLACH

41 CORDELL HULL LAKE

Description: Forests of chinkapin oak, blue ash, and red cedar line the banks of the Cumberland River. From the visitor center at dam, view white-tailed deer, occasional common loon or bufflehead in winter, osprey during migration. Equestrians may view wild turkey, resident Canada geese, bald eagles, and black racers along level, ten-mile lakeshore trail at Holleman's Bend.

Viewing Information: Try viewing with a spotting scope offered at visitor center, or hike the Turkey Creek Trail near dam. *PLEASE VIEW FROM AUTO ONLY DURING HUNTING SEASON, SEPTEMBER-FEBRUARY, AT HOLLEMAN'S BEND; OTHERWISE WEAR BLAZE ORANGE.*

Directions: *From Interstate 40 east of Nashville (fifty miles) take exit 258.* **To reach dam:** *proceed north six miles on TN 53 to Carthage. Turn north on TN 263 to entrance road; follow signs to resource manager office/visitor center.* **To reach Holleman's Bend:** *travel north on TN 53 for 4.1 miles. Turn right on US 70N, proceed for 7.9 miles. Left on TN 53, continue 5.8 miles. Park on left at Holleman's Bend Road, or drive to boat landing at end of Holleman's Bend Road.*

Ownership: USACOE (615) 735-1034; managed in cooperation with TWRA (615) 858-2995 or (800) 262-6704
Size: 1,550 acres   **Closest Town:** Carthage, Gainesboro

42 STANDING STONE STATE PARK, FOREST AND WMA

Description: This scenic spot is a favorite of birders and wildflower enthusiasts. Moist forest floors harbor abundant salamanders and wildflowers in late March and April. Ten warbler species nest here, including the yellow, cerulean, pine, Kentucky, black-and-white, hooded, and northern parula.

Viewing Information: Maps, brochures available at state park office. Access from ten miles of marked trails and rental rowboats. Paved road leading downhill to Standing Stone Lake excellent for warblers and wildflowers in spring. Lake and smaller ponds feature waterfowl in winter. *USE CAUTION DURING STATEWIDE DEER HUNTING SEASONS ON WMA.*

Directions: *From junction of TN 52 and TN 42 north of Livingston travel 8.8 miles north on TN 52. Turn south on TN 136 and travel 1.3 miles to park entrance. Continue 0.6 miles to park office.*

Ownership: TDEC/BPR (615) 823-6347; TDF (615) 526-9502; TWRA (615) 484-9571 or (800) 262-6704
Size: 10,000 acres state forest; 1,000 acres state park
Closest Town: Livingston

43 DALE HOLLOW LAKE

Description: WOA. Dale Hollow Lake on the Obey River is one of the state's best places to view wintering bald eagles. Up to seventy eagles winter here annually, feasting on fish and injured waterfowl. Diving ducks are another winter attraction; watch for lesser scaup, bufflehead, ring-necked duck, and goldeneye. Osprey present in spring. Visitors may glimpse river otter or mink. Occasional stopover point for migrating sandhill cranes.

Viewing Information: High probability of viewing a diversity of waterfowl, including hooded mergansers, loons, and coots October through March; wood ducks seen year-round. High probability of seeing bald eagles October through March—best viewing in vicinity of 7.3-mile trail between Willow Grove and Lillydale Recreation Areas on south side of the lake. Public eagle viewing tours offered each January by USACOE. Maps, information available from resource manager's office. Viewing from a boat allows more opportunities than from shoreline, but is not necessary. Twenty-two public access points serve the lake; eighteen are in Tennessee. Spotting scope suggested. Visit adjacent national fish hatchery. *USE CAUTION DURING WINTER HUNTING SEASON; INQUIRE AT RESOURCE MANAGER'S OFFICE FOR DATES, LOCATIONS.*

Directions: *From Interstate 40 east of Nashville, take exit 280 (Baxter/Gainesboro). Travel north on TN 56 through Gainesboro. Turn north onto TN 53, proceed through Celina and follow signs to resource manager's office.*

Ownership: USACOE (615) 243-3136
Size: 27,000-acre lake; 24,000 acres of land   **Closest Town:** Celina

The musical honking of resident Canada geese is now a familiar sound at many reservoirs and parks in Tennessee. The elegant male gander is a feisty protector of the nest during breeding season.   LEONARD LEE RUE III

EASTERN MOUNTAINS AND VALLEYS

Cherokee National Forest   LARRY ULRICH

The Eastern Mountains and Valleys include three distinct geographic areas: the Cumberland Plateau, the Ridge and Valley, and the Unaka Mountains of the Southern Appalachians (see map below).

Averaging about 2,000 feet above sea level, the rugged Cumberland Plateau is cut by deep gorges and topped by mountains rising to about 3500 feet in elevation. The limestone bedrock here is covered by a thick sandstone cap featuring prominent cliffs and water-falls. Extensive coalfields in this region have been mined, particularly during the past century. Caves are abundant, and the Plateau's limestones are connected to the bedrock of the Mammoth Cave system of Kentucky. Specially adapted cave wildlife include the blind Tennessee cave salamander and the federally listed endangered gray and Indiana bats.

To the east, the folding and fracturing of the earth during periods of mountain building activity has created row after row of broad valleys separated by the knifelike parallel ridges of the Ridge and Valley region. Landscape characteristics include

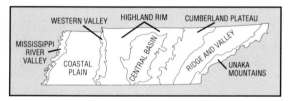

second growth hardwood forests rimmed with pine ridgetops and intensively developed agriculture in the valleys, intermingled with urban and industrial development at a scale unmatched elsewhere in the state. The Eastern Tennessee River and many of its tributaries, including the Powell, Clinch, Holston, and French Broad rivers are now impounded by a network of locks and dams.

The rugged high mountains of Tennessee's eastern border—publicly owned,

sparsely populated, and heavily forested—hold hope for the survival of the black bear, cougar, and the red wolf. Within the Unaka Mountains of the Southern Appalachians, Tennessee's highest peak, Clingman's Dome, stands at 6,642 feet above sea level. Dramatic variations in elevation, temperature and rainfall have created a diverse ecosystem, including red spruce and Fraser fir forests and treeless high elevation balds. Cool, wet cove forests, known for towering hemlocks, tulip poplars and umbrella magnolias, are home to record numbers of amphibians, especially salamanders, and the greatest variety of plants anywhere in North America.

Red Wolf   JACK WINFIELD ROSS

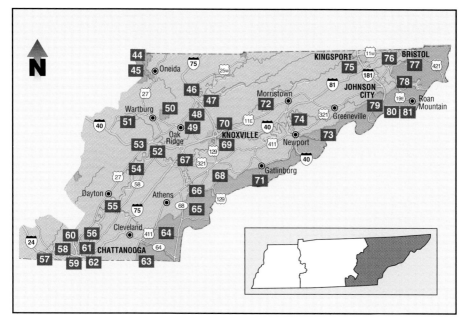

Wildlife Viewing Sites

44 Pickett State Park
and State Forest

45 Big South Fork National
River and Recreation Area

46 Cove Lake State
Recreational Area

47 Norris Dam Reservation

48 Eagle Bend Fish Hatchery

49 University of Tennessee
Arboretum

50 Frozen Head State Park
and Natural Area

51 Catoosa Wildlife
Management Area

52 Kingston Steam Plant

53 Mount Roosevelt Wildlife
Management Area

54 Watts Bar Lake

55 Blythe Ferry Unit,
Hiwassee Refuge

56 Chickamauga Lake

57 Nickajack Cave Refuge

58 Raccoon Mountain
Pumped-Storage Plant

59 Reflection Riding/
Chattanooga Nature Center

60 Signal Point Park

61 Brainerd Levee

62 Audubon Acres

63 Cherokee National Forest:
Conasauga River

64 Hiwassee State Scenic River

65 Cherokee National Forest:
Tellico Auto Loop

66 Chota Peninsula of
Tellico Lake WMA

67 Fort Loudoun Dam-
Tellico Dam Reservation

68 Foothills Parkway
(Western Section)

69 Ijams Nature Center-
Eastern State WMA

70 Sharps Ridge

71 Great Smoky Mountains
National Park

72 Panther Creek State Park

73 Cherokee National Forest:
Weaver's Bend

74 Rankin Bottoms

75 Bays Mountain Park

76 Steele Creek Park

77 Cherokee National Forest: Little
Oak Watchable Wildlife Area

78 Wilbur Lake

79 Erwin National Fish Hatchery-
Unicoi County Heritage Museum

80 Cherokee National Forest:
Unaka Mountain Auto Tour

81 Highlands of Roan Mountain

44 PICKETT STATE PARK, STATE FOREST, AND WMA

Description: Rhododendron-laced forests and geologic wonders enhance wildlife viewing at this beautiful site. The small-footed and Rafinesque's big-eared bat are seen here. Diverse flora includes the endangered Cumberland sandwort. Such migratory birds as the whip-poor-will, ruby-throated hummingbird, wood thrush, and worm-eating and hooded warbler are present spring and fall, and through the summer nesting season. The sandstone "rockhouses," arches, and dripping clifflines are home to luminescent glow worms, green salamanders, and spotted skunks.

Viewing Information: A popular summer program features a tour of rockhouse fauna, including a nighttime visit inside Hazard Cave to view glow worms. Watch migrating hawks in fall from Kentucky View Overlook. Canoe cliff-lined Arch Lake, which teems with red-spotted newts. Eastern phoebes and rough-winged swallows nest on rock faces. Check sandy soils for tracks of nocturnal mammals. Sixty-four miles of park foot trails connect with adjacent Big South Fork NRRA (site 45). *HUNTING DURING LATE FALL DEER SEASON ON WMA; HIKERS USE CAUTION. CHECK WITH PARK OFFICE FOR INFORMATION.*

Directions: *From junction of TN 154 and TN 297 north of Jamestown, travel north 3.7 miles on TN 154 to state park entrance and office. Hazard Cave and Indian Rockhouse are 0.7 miles south of entrance.*

Ownership: TDEC/BPR (615) 879-5821; TDF (615) 526-9502;
TWRA (615) 484-9571 or (800) 262-6704
Size: State forest, 10,887 acres; state park, 865 acres; WMA, 11,000 acres
Closest Town: Jamestown

Shallow overhangs of sandstone, known locally as "rockhouses," have provided shelter for a wide variety of mammals, birds, salamanders, and even humans over the centuries. Hazard Cave is one of the best known rockhouses in the state.

STATE OF TENNESSEE:
TOURIST DEVELOPMENT

45 BIG SOUTH FORK NATIONAL RIVER AND RECREATION AREA

Description: Remote, rugged, and wild, Big South Fork was first accessed by paved highway in 1983. Waters of the Big South Fork of the Cumberland and its tributaries are home to nearly seventy fish species, including colorful darters and Tennessee muskellunge. Formerly home to forty-four mussel species. Black bear may be reintroduced here.

Viewing Information: Explore the dripping sandstone cliffs for their unique, specially-adapted flora and fauna, including eastern phoebes, eastern woodrats and their acorn caches or "middens," as well as salamanders and orb weavers. Moderate probability of seeing white-tailed deer and reintroduced wild turkey near East Rim, also ruffed grouse, raccoons, and bats. Coyote, wild boar, mink and reintroduced river otter less likely. Try auto tours to Twin Arches, Bandy Creek, and East Rim overlook; check overlooks for migrating raptors on sunny September and October afternoons. Bandy Creek Visitor Center has maps, species lists, and general information. Public programs offered seasonally. Excellent canoe viewing. *PUBLIC HUNTING PERMITTED; EXERCISE CAUTION DURING FALL DEER AND SPRING TURKEY HUNTING SEASONS. CONSULT VISITOR CENTER FOR HUNTING DATES AND LOCATIONS, AND FOR WHITEWATER SAFETY PRECAUTIONS BEFORE VENTURING INTO RIVER. RESCUES ARE DIFFICULT IN REMOTE TERRAIN.*

Directions: *From junction of US 27 and TN 297 in Oneida, proceed west 12.5 miles on TN 297 to Bandy Creek Visitor Center.*

Ownership: NPS (615) 879-3625
Size: 106,000 acres   **Closest Town:** Oneida, Jamestown

Mink are most likely seen in remote places like Big South Fork of the Cumberland River, where their movements can be less guarded. These sleek predators are solitary and active throughout the year.
JOHN GERLACH

63

ENDANGERED SPECIES
IN TENNESSEE

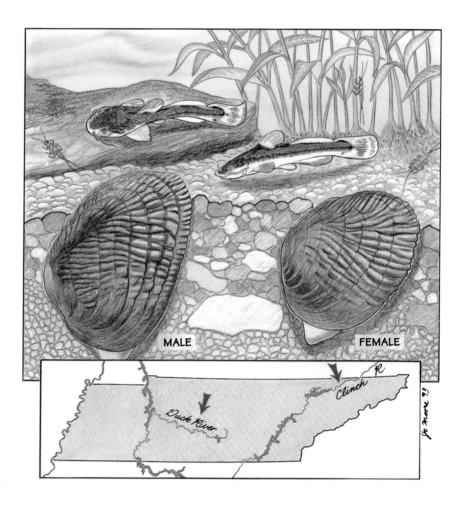

MALE   FEMALE

More federally-listed endangered species of plants and animals live in Tennessee than in any other inland state. Endangered species are living things that could disappear from the earth forever. Many are freshwater mussels and fish; about one-fourth of Tennessee's native fish species are in trouble. A rare, tiny catfish, the pygmy madtom (pictured above), lives only in portions of the Clinch and Duck rivers. The endangered birdwing pearlymussel (above) occurs here, and in sections of the Elk and Powell rivers. Their distribution over such a small area makes them extremely vulnerable to excessive harvest, pollution, river channelization and impoundment.

Often the best way to conserve a species is to protect habitat, or to save an entire ecosystem. Many viewing areas in this guide provide habitat for rare species, including sites 1, 32, 57, and 63. Endangered plants and animals in Tennessee need your help.

46 COVE LAKE STATE RECREATIONAL AREA

Description: WOA. Cove Lake has nearly filled with silt, creating one of the largest freshwater marsh habitats in east Tennessee. Wetland wildlife found here includes the great blue heron, beaver, belted kingfisher, tree swallow, and raccoon. Spring and fall, look for shorebirds at lake's north end, American woodcock in low wet woods. Songbirds such as the common yellowthroat, orchard oriole, and indigo bunting best seen April through September. Check dead standing trees in lake for woodpeckers. Abundant turtles, including snappers and red-eared sliders.

Viewing Information: Site is heavily used during weekends, especially in summer; undeveloped portion is excellent for wildlife viewing. Try the observation platform near picnic area, also the trail to Buckeye Spring. Guided tours in summer. Information at park office. Good viewing of waterfowl, primarily mallards, wood ducks, resident and migratory Canada geese; sixteen species possible in winter. View hooded mergansers on lake south of US 25W.

Directions: *From Interstate 75 exit 134 north of Knoxville, travel east on US 25W for one mile and turn left into park entrance.*

Ownership: TDEC/BPR (615) 562-8355
Size: 713 acres **Closest Town:** Caryville

47 NORRIS DAM RESERVATION

Description: WOA. River Bluff Trail, a 3.2-mile loop, features Celandine poppies, squirrel corn, Dutchman's breeches and trout lily in spring bloom. Songbird Trail features both native, non-native plantings for wildlife. Watch for orchard and northern orioles, eastern bluebirds and tree swallows below the dam.

Viewing Information: View from hiking trails on Dam Reservation and adjacent State Park. Free trail brochure available from TVA. Paved Edge Path on Reservation (one-quarter mile) offers barrier-free access. Moderate probability of white-tailed deer along roadsides year-round at dawn and dusk. High probability for songbirds, especially migratory species, spring and fall. Introduced rainbow and brown trout stocked below dam; watch for great blue herons, green-backed herons, and gulls in winter. Adjacent Norris Dam State Park offers hiking, barge tours, occasional cave tours, lodging, and facilities.

Directions: *From Interstate 75 north of Knoxville, take exit 122 (Norris/Clinton). Right (east) on TN 61 for 1.4 miles. Left on US 441 for four miles to TVA's Norris Dam Reservation. Proceed another three miles to Norris Dam State Resort Park.*

Ownership: TVA (800) TVA-LAND; TDEC\BPR (615) 426-7461
Size: 822 acres **Closest Town:** Norris

48 EAGLE BEND FISH HATCHERY

Description: WOA. Fields along banks of the Clinch River punctuated by shallow warmwater hatchery ponds provide habitat for migratory shorebirds spring and fall, such as ruddy turnstones, greater and lesser yellowlegs, common snipe; waders like great blue, green-backed and black-crowned night herons, great, snowy and cattle egrets; and an occasional flock of bobolinks in spring. Ponds not in use support tempting moist-soil vegetation. Shallow ponds support bass, crappie, walleye, sauger, in addition to watersnakes, map turtles, sliders. Listen for spring peepers, chorus frogs, and gray treefrogs.

Viewing Information: Best viewing for shorebirds such as least sandpipers April-May, August-September, by auto or on foot. Water levels of ponds variable; conditions for shorebirds also fluctuate. Muskrats and woodchucks common in warmer months. Red-winged blackbirds numerous year-round; savannah, song, and swamp sparrows common in winter. *VIEWING ON WEEKDAYS ONLY. WEEKEND VIEWING ON SPECIAL REQUEST FROM GROUPS. STOP AT OFFICE, ALERT STAFF TO YOUR ARRIVAL; GATES ARE CLOSED SPORADICALLY. DRIVE CAUTIOUSLY ALONG GRASSED LEVEE BANKS.*

Directions: *From Knoxville, north on Interstate 75 to exit 122 (Clinton/Norris). Proceed west on TN 61 for 3.7 miles, cross Clinch River, take immediate left.*

Ownership: TWRA (615) 457-5135
Size: 100 acres   **Closest Town:** Clinton

49 UNIVERSITY OF TENNESSEE ARBORETUM

Description: WOA. Nestled within 2,260-acre Oak Ridge Forest, this arboretum is only one part of a research, education, and demonstration project of the University's Forestry Experiment Stations. Visitors can explore upland hardwood and pine forests, small ponds, and an extensive collection of over 800 species of plants. Demonstration area features backyard wildlife plantings. Watch for eastern bluebirds and white-breasted nuthatches year-round.

Viewing Information: View from 2.5 miles of interpretive trails. Access roads available to elderly, handicapped on request. High probability of viewing white-tailed deer and nesting songbirds, including prairie and pine warblers, eastern phoebes, and orchard orioles. Moderate probability of seeing red-tailed hawks, other raptors, and small mammals year-round. Visitor center (open weekdays) offers maps, checklists. Some group tours on request. Annual activities sponsored by Arboretum Society.

Directions: *From downtown Oak Ridge, travel three miles southeast on TN 62 to the signed entrance of Forestry Experiment Station on left.*

Ownership: University of Tennessee (615) 483-3571
Size: 250 acres   **Closest Town:** Oak Ridge

50 FROZEN HEAD STATE PARK AND NATURAL AREA

Description: A protected area within the state's coalfield, Frozen Head is a unique spot of rich cove and upland hardwood forests atop the divide between the Cumberland and Tennessee River watersheds. Here is the state's, and one of the country's, most important breeding spots for cerulean warblers. At elevations up to 3,300 feet, Frozen Head also features Tennessee's westernmost breeding spot for veeries and chestnut-sided, Canada, black-throated blue, and blackburnian warblers. Mammals include white-tailed deer, flying squirrels, and spotted skunks. Curious viewers may find spotted, red, spring, and rare Black Mountain dusky salamanders, abundant red efts. Wondrous displays of spring wildflowers and fall colors are an extra attraction, as are Debord and Emory Gap Falls.

Viewing Information: More than fifty miles of challenging foot trails lead into remote backcountry. Highest probability for breeding warblers in June; watch for parent hooded, black-and-white, and cerulean warblers, and ovenbirds feeding young unaffected by parasitic brown-headed cowbirds on almost any trail. Woodchucks, gray squirrels, and gray foxes during warmer months. Observe timber rattlesnakes on sandstone outcrops at Chimney Top from a safe distance. Visitor center offers information, maps, guided tours. No view in the state is more instructive than that from the fire tower on Frozen Head Mountain.

Directions: *From junction of US 27 and TN 62 in Wartburg, proceed 2.1 miles east on TN 62. Turn left (north) on Flat Fork Road, continue four miles on Flat Fork Road to park entrance.*

Ownership: TDEC/BPR (615) 346-3318
Size: 11,869 acres
Closest Town: Wartburg

Nesting colonies of cerulean warblers are found only in the high canopy of a few stands of big timber in Tennessee, including the forests of Frozen Head State Park. These "neotropical migrants" spend the winter in South America's Andes Mountains.

B. SCHORRE/VIREO

51 CATOOSA WILDLIFE MANAGEMENT AREA

Description: This gently rolling Cumberland Plateau terrain is the site of extensive management efforts to benefit white-tailed deer, wild turkeys, bob-white quail, and other game animals. The highlight of the area, difficult to access along much of its length, is the remote, rugged and challenging canyon of the National Wild and Scenic Obed River, home to a federally endangered mussel, the state threatened river otter, and occasional osprey or peregrine falcon. A segment of the river is designated critical habitat for a federally threatened fish, the spotfin chub. Forests are primarily of hardwoods; modest acreages of shortleaf pine forest formerly harbored a small population of federally endangered red-cockaded woodpeckers. White-tailed deer, wild turkeys, ruffed grouse often seen; occasional screech or great-horned owl. Largest landholding of TWRA.

Viewing Information: Maps available from TWRA. Predominant activity is hunting. Auto viewing, hiking on 110 miles gravel roads; 150 miles of trails, old logging roads. Secluded and remote experiences. *AREA CLOSED TO ALL PUBLIC ACCESS JANUARY 31 - APRIL 1. ACCESS TO HUNTERS ONLY DURING BIG GAME HUNTS; CHECK HUNTING REGULATIONS PUBLISHED BY TWRA FOR SPECIFIC DATES, ADDITIONAL INFORMATION. PARK ALONG ROADSIDES, BUT DO NOT BLOCK ENTRY TO GATED ROADS OR TO FIELDS.* Call NPS office for information on Obed River access.

Directions: *From Interstate 40 take Genesis Road exit east of Crossville. Travel north eight miles on Genesis Road to entrance.*

Ownership: TWRA (615) 484-9571, (800) 262-6704; NPS (615) 346-6295
Size: 80,000 acres   **Closest Town:** Crossville

The male ruffed grouse anchors himself with sharp claws to a carefully chosen log and beats his wings rapidly, creating a sound that resembles an escalating heartbeat. To locate a "drumming" grouse, move towards the bird only while it sounds off—be sure to halt when the drumming stops.
LEONARD LEE RUE III

52 KINGSTON STEAM PLANT

Description: WOA. The shallow wetlands and mudflats of settling ponds here are renowned statewide as shorebird viewing hotspots spring and fall. Over thirty species may be seen here—sanderlings, short-billed dowitchers, greater yellowlegs, eight sandpiper species, and occasional rarities such as piping plover, northern phalarope, and the Hudsonian godwit.

Viewing Information: A spotting scope is strongly recommended for best viewing. Search all ponds for a combination of shallow water and mudflats; water levels fluctuate daily. In winter, many waterfowl species are present, along with flocks of song, swamp, and savannah sparrows. Summertime brings squadrons of dragonflies. Watch for peregrine falcons during migration. Red-shouldered hawks and a resident population of giant Canada geese are present year-round.

Directions: *From the junction of TN 58 south and US 70 in Kingston, travel 2.2 miles west on US 70. Turn right on Swan Pond Road at Kingston Steam Plant sign and travel 1.5 miles. Turn right into parking area beside ballfield and walk uphill to reach pond levees.*

Ownership: TVA (800) TVA-LAND
Size: 400 acres   **Closest Town:** Kingston

53 MOUNT ROOSEVELT WMA

Description: WOA. The hardwood and pine forests of Walden's Ridge form a panoramic background for observing daytime hawk and songbird migrations, particularly in autumn. Thousands of broad-winged and red-tailed hawks, turkey and black vultures, northern flickers, and blue jays stream past in September and October. Easier to overlook but no less amazing are the numbers of butterflies, particularly monarchs, that ride the same winds southward.

Viewing Information: *SEASONAL SITE.* Optimal viewing with spotting scope or binoculars. High probability of viewing raptors, songbirds, and monarch butterflies from overlook or fire tower during warm mid-day hours in September and October. Check treetops or exposed branches along ridgetop road for resting birds. Spur trail near fire tower leads to Walden Ridge Trail. *USE CAUTION DURING STATEWIDE HUNTING SEASONS.* Maps and information available by calling TWRA.

Directions: *From junction of US 70 and US 27 in Rockwood, travel west on US 70 for 2.2 miles. Turn right at Mount Roosevelt State Forest sign and travel 1.5 miles to fire tower and overlook.*

Ownership: TWRA (615) 484-9571 or (800) 262-6704
Size: 11,000 acres   **Closest Town:** Rockwood

54 WATTS BAR LAKE

Description: For reasons unknown, this main-stem Tennessee River impoundment with 783 miles of shoreline has the largest inland nesting population of ospreys in the Southeast. Possible explanations include the lake's depth, or the birds' willingness to use manmade nesting structures. Whatever the reason, the lake is host each spring to a large population of "fish hawks."

Viewing Information: Ospreys nest May-July, concentrated between the Euchee boat dock on River Road and Thief Neck Island. Best viewing is from a boat; many launch ramps are available. Obtain map by contacting TVA or TWRA. *PLEASE VIEW OSPREY NESTS FROM A DISTANCE; USE BINOCULARS AND BE SENSITIVE TO SIGNS OF DISTRESS.* Concentrations of great blue herons, black-crowned night herons, and great egrets may be seen near Long Island. Waterfowl and bald eagles are common in winter. *USE CAUTION DURING HUNTING SEASONS NOVEMBER-JANUARY; DO NOT APPROACH OCCUPIED DUCK BLINDS. PAINT ROCK REFUGE CLOSED TO PUBLIC OCTOBER 15-FEBRUARY 1.* Public lands of Watts Bar Reservoir Reservation are home to white-tailed deer, raccoon, woodchuck, muskrat, and fox, as well as mink, skunk, and coyote.

Directions: *From US 70 in Kingston, take TN 58 south 3.6 miles to River Road (TN 304). Turn right, following River Road along east shore of the lake. Alternatively, from Rockwood take US 27/TN 29 south to Spring City for access to west shore. Thief Neck Marina is accessed by Valley and Winton Chapel Roads.*

Ownership: TVA (800) TVA-LAND; portions managed in cooperation with TWRA (615) 484-9571 or (800) 262-6704
Size: 38,900-acre lake is seventy-two miles long
Closest Town: Kingston, Rockwood, Spring City

Beginning in the mid-1970s, TWRA, TVA, and many volunteers have installed nest platforms and assisted with an osprey reintroduction program at Watts Bar Lake. Watch these "fish hawks" hover until a fish nears the surface, then dive feet-first to seize the prey in their talons.
JOHN GERLACH

Description: WOA. These mudflats, croplands and ponds near the confluence of the Tennessee and Hiwassee Rivers offer outstanding views of large numbers of waterfowl, but the real wildlife spectacle here is migrating sandhill cranes. From November through late March, up to 5,000 of these regal, slate-gray birds rest and feed on the refuge, the only sizeable gathering of cranes between Florida and their northern nesting grounds. With a seven-foot wingspan and loud, trumpeting call, sandhill cranes offer a memorable viewing experience. Twenty waterfowl species may also be observed here in winter; most abundant are mallards and black ducks, and Canada geese.

Viewing Information: Optimal views of sandhill cranes with a spotting scope. High probability of viewing cranes and waterfowl throughout winter, with best viewing in March. Bald eagles and northern harriers also visit in winter. During site's open months, travel on foot along gravel roads and pastures toward Chickamauga Lake. Look for cranes feeding and resting on Hiwassee Island, in corn fields, or in flight. *PLEASE OBSERVE CRANES FROM A DISTANCE.* Plans are underway to build an observation tower here for year-round viewing. *AREA OPEN ONLY TO HUNTERS DURING LIMITED SMALL AND BIG GAME SEASONS; INQUIRE WITH TWRA FOR DATES. CURRENTLY LIMITED ACCESS OCTOBER 15-FEBRUARY 28.*

Directions: *From junction of TN 58 and TN 60 near Georgetown, follow TN 60 7.8 miles north. Turn right onto Meigs County Road 131, proceed one-half mile to first gravel road, turn left. Parking at 0.8 miles, at end of road.*

Ownership: TVA; managed by TWRA (615) 484-9571 or (800) 262-6704
Size: 1,000 acres   **Closest Town:** Birchwood, Dayton

Listen for the trumpeting "kar-r-r-o-o-o" of the sandhill crane overhead, sometimes from great heights. Flocks of cranes winter and rest in Tennessee as they migrate between breeding grounds in the remote Arctic and wintering grounds mostly to the south.

BILL LEA

56 CHICKAMAUGA LAKE

Description: WOA. Diverse and abundant wildlife inhabit the urban sanctuaries and greenways encircling lower Chickamauga Lake near Chattanooga, demonstrating the benefits of reserving forests that connect habitats of streams, ridges, and large reservoirs, providing wildlife with important travel routes. A sampling of Chickamauga's many viewing opportunities begins with **North Chickamauga Creek Greenway,** offering a scenic paved creekside trail and views of great blue herons, kingfishers, and turtles. Next is the **Big Ridge TVA Small Wild Area,** accessed from the greenway, with a 1.3-mile loop trail through 100-year-old upland forest. Watch for abundant songbirds, pileated woodpeckers, black racer snakes, and wildflowers such as yellow trillium, and federally-listed large-flowered skullcaps. At **Chester Frost Park,** stands of pine are the year-round home of brown-headed nuthatches and red-headed woodpeckers. Shorelines offer views of osprey, lesser yellowlegs, and spotted sandpipers during migration. The **Booker T. Washington State Park** shelters twenty species of waterfowl, including the greater scaup, common loon, ring-necked duck, coots, and grebes. The mudflats of **Savannah Bay** are popular viewing sites for wading birds and songbirds. Sandpipers, plovers, and other shorebirds are abundant when the lake drawdown coincides with spring and fall migrations. This is also the northernmost wintering area for dunlin in the interior US.

Viewing Information: North Chickamauga Creek Greenway: Barrier-free trail access from picnic pavillion; **Big Ridge Trail** accessed from upper loop of paved trail. Best birding spring through fall; wildflowers peak in spring. *DO NOT COLLECT OR DISTURB PLANTS.* **Chester Frost Park:** Birding from shoreline and from trails; binoculars or spotting scope strongly recommended. *DO NOT APPROACH DUCK HUNTING BLINDS DURING OPEN WINTER SEASON. CROWDS LIKELY ON WEEKENDS SPRING-FALL.* On-site restrooms, camping, boat ramp. **Booker T. Washington State Park:** Daylight viewing only. View from bluff and woodland trail or from auto along shoreline roads. Use a spotting scope for best views of waterfowl. Restrooms and boat ramp on site. **Savannah Bay:** Best viewing areas are boat landing on Snow Hill Road, parking area east of Roy Lane Bridge, and along shoreline trail paralleling Snow Hill Road; best viewing October - April. *USE CAUTION DURING WINTER WATERFOWL HUNTING SEASON. PLEASE RESPECT RIGHTS OF PRIVATE LANDOWNERS.* No facilities.

Directions: *See map, opposite page.*

Ownership: Big Ridge TVA Small Wild Area: TVA (800) TVA-LAND; **Chester Frost Park:** TVA; Hamilton County Parks and Recreation (615) 842-0177; **Booker T. Washington State Park:** TDEC/BPR (615) 894-4955; **Savannah Bay:** TVA, managed in cooperation with TWRA (615) 587-7037 or (800) 262-6704.
Size: NA   **Closest Town:** Chattanooga

Facilities and Recreation: *See Viewing Information*

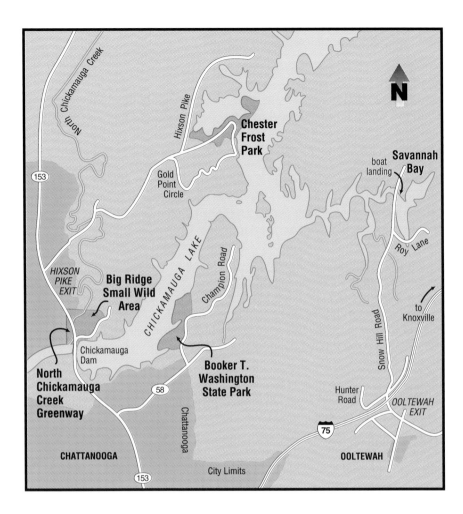

The deeper waters of Tennessee's reservoirs are winter haunts of "divers" such as ring-necked ducks. The ring on the bill is a better field mark than the ring on the neck.
JOHN GERLACH

57 | NICKAJACK CAVE REFUGE

Description: WOA. Forested limestone slopes shelter this important cave, home to a summer population of over 50,000 federally endangered female gray bats and their young. These voracious insect-eaters, each consuming over 3,000 flying insects every night, choose only a few large caves with high domes and adjacent water for their nursery colonies. Gray bats cluster within the dome by day to generate body heat that aids development of their young. This dark habitat also supports blind Tennessee cave salamanders, and small numbers of hibernating Indiana and eastern small-footed bats in winter, after the gray bats have migrated. Green salamanders cling to the cliffs with padded toes. Also watch for cliff swallows tending mud nests attached to the cliff face.

Viewing Information: A state-designated Wildlife Observation Area and Refuge. *OPEN APRIL 1 THROUGH OCTOBER 15. PUBLIC ACCESS ONTO TRAIL AND VIEWING PLATFORM ONLY; ACCESS INTO CAVE PROHIBITED.* Platform offers a high probability of viewing exit flight of gray bats within one hour of dark each night, late April through early October. Morning return is less concentrated. Moderate probability of viewing waterfowl, including double-crested cormorants, in winter.

Directions: *From Interstate 24 west of Chattanooga, take exit 161 (Haletown/New Hope). Turn north (left) onto TN 156 and travel five miles to TVA Maple View Public Use Area. Viewing platform is 0.25-mile down path from parking area.*

Ownership: TVA (800) TVA-LAND; managed in cooperation with TWRA (615) 484-9571 or (800)262-6704

Size: NA **Closest Town:** South Pittsburg

MERLIN D. TUTTLE/
BAT CONSERVATION
INTERNATIONAL

STATE OF TENNESSEE: TOURIST DEVELOPMENT

Almost all of the gray bats in existence hibernate in eight individual caves. These highly specific habitat requirements make their existence a tenuous one.

58 RACCOON MOUNTAIN PUMPED-STORAGE PLANT

Description: WOA. Raccoon Mountain sits on the rim of the Tennessee River Gorge, the Grand Canyon of Tennessee. Bald eagles visit this mountaintop reservoir in winter, attracted by fish injured in pumping process. Plentiful hawks ride the winds south in autumn, including broad-winged, Cooper's, sharp-shinned, and red-tailed hawks, as well as osprey and northern harrier.

Viewing Information: *SEASONAL VIEWING.* Binoculars or a spotting scope are strongly recommended here. A variety of waterfowl, including common loons in fall and winter, may easily be seen from road encircling reservoir. Organized hawk watches led by Chattanooga Chapter of the Tennessee Ornithological Society are held each autumn at TVA visitor center overlook. Best viewing mid-September to October, at mid-day, following the passage of a cold front or during prevailing northwesterly winds. Also try overlook near microwave tower.

Directions: *From Interstate 24 west of Chattanooga, take exit 174. Travel 2.5 miles northwest on US Routes 41N/64W/72W. Turn right at pumped storage plant sign. Travel 8.2 miles, following signs to visitor center.*

Ownership: TVA (800) TVA-LAND
Size: 530 acres   **Closest Town:** Chattanooga

59 REFLECTION RIDING/CHATTANOOGA NATURE CENTER

Description: Nature center offers a variety of programs and activities, including canoe trips and wild cave tours. A barrier-free boardwalk through remnant wetland forest on Lookout Creek offers views of such reptiles as banded watersnakes and pond sliders. Also look for great crested and acadian flycatchers, and prothonotary and Kentucky warblers in summer. Listen for barred owls and pileated woodpeckers. Beaver and muskrat are present year-round.

Viewing Information: Great blue and green-backed herons, and egrets most abundant summer and fall. White-tailed deer and larger predators like raccoon, coyote, and fox may be seen occasionally. Observant visitors may spot a flying squirrel. Spring wildflowers in uplands. Three-mile auto tour passes through Reflection Riding Nature Preserve. Extensive system of walking trails.

Directions: *From Interstate 24 in west Chattanooga, take exit 175 (Brown's Ferry Road) and turn left (south). Travel 0.5 miles, turn left onto Cummings Highway, and travel 0.7 miles. Turn right on Old Wauhatchie Pike, then take an immediate right onto Garden Road. Continue 1.1 miles to Nature Center.*

Ownership: PVT: Chattanooga Nature Center (615) 821-1160
Size: 300 acres   **Closest Town:** Chattanooga

60 SIGNAL POINT PARK

Description: WOA. Perched 1,000 feet above the Tennessee River, the unobstructed views from this brow of the gorge are ideal for watching "kettles," or spiraling concentrations of raptors, in the fall. Among thirteen species recorded at this site, broad-winged and red-tailed hawks, as well as black and turkey vultures are most conspicuous. Cooper's hawks and peregrine falcons may also be seen.

Viewing Information: *SEASONAL VIEWING, BEST ON SUNNY AFTERNOONS IN LATE SEPTEMBER, OCTOBER.* Spotting scope strongly recommended. Take a short path to the well-maintained overlook, the site of a Civil War signalling point. Expect crowds on weekends.

Directions: *From US 27 in north Chattanooga, follow US 127 north to town of Signal Mountain. Turn left onto Signal Mountain Boulevard, follow signs to site.*

Ownership: NPS (615) 821-7786
Size: Five acres
Closest Town: Signal Mountain

61 BRAINERD LEVEE

Description: WOA. Mudflats and a small freshwater marsh of sedges, cattails and willows adjacent to this flood-control levee can host abundant great blue, little blue and green-backed herons, also great egrets, May-September. Watch for common snipe and waterfowl in winter. Blue-winged teal are frequent during migration in April and September-November. The wet fields and edges support nesting willow flycatchers and grasshopper sparrows. Beaver and muskrat inhabit the adjacent oxbows. The snail darter, a federally-listed fish, was rediscovered in South Chickamauga Creek in 1980 after it was thought to be extinct.

Viewing Information: *SEASONAL VIEWING.* Access along paved trail atop 2.6 mile-long levee. Late afternoon viewing is best, after sun drops below treeline. Occasional rarities here include the white ibis, and pectoral and solitary sandpiper. *HIGH WATER LEVELS PROVIDE BEST VIEWING.*

Directions: *From Chattanooga, take Interstate 75 north to exit 4, TN 153. Travel north on TN 153 to Shallowford Road Exit. Turn left (west) on Shallowford Road, travel two miles to intersection of Shallowford and North Moore roads. Parking lot is at the corner.*

Ownership: City of Chattanooga (615) 757-4963
Size: 110 acres
Closest Town: Chattanooga

Description: Surrounded by urban Chattanooga, Audubon Acres offers a quiet stroll among giant shortleaf pine, beech and other hardwood trees, and excellent birding at the edge of South Chickamauga Creek.

Viewing Information: View along ten miles of well-maintained trails through upland and bottomland forests. Numerous special events take place at this site, listed on the National Register of Historic Places as the home of Native American naturalist Spring Frog. Abundant wildflowers in season, including mayapple, trillium, and columbine; spectacular displays of Virginia bluebell in early May. Excellent observation of migratory birds. Moderate probability of viewing raccoon, muskrat, gray fox, and woodchuck. Site is focus for guided programs to several other locations in the metropolitan area, including MacLellan Island. Newsletter and events flyer available on request.

Directions: From Chattanooga, take Interstate 75 north to East Brainerd Road exit 3A. Go east on East Brainerd Road (TN 320) 0.9 mile, then turn right onto Gunbarrel Road and travel one mile. Turn right on Sanctuary Road and follow signs 0.5 mile to entrance at end of road.

Ownership: Chattanooga Audubon Society (615) 892-1499
Size: 130 acres   **Closest Town:** Chattanooga

Little blue herons disperse widely from their nesting colonies at the end of the summer breeding season, when they are likely to appear at small marshes like Brainerd Levee.

JOHN GERLACH

THE AQUATIC DIVERSITY OF EAST TENNESSEE

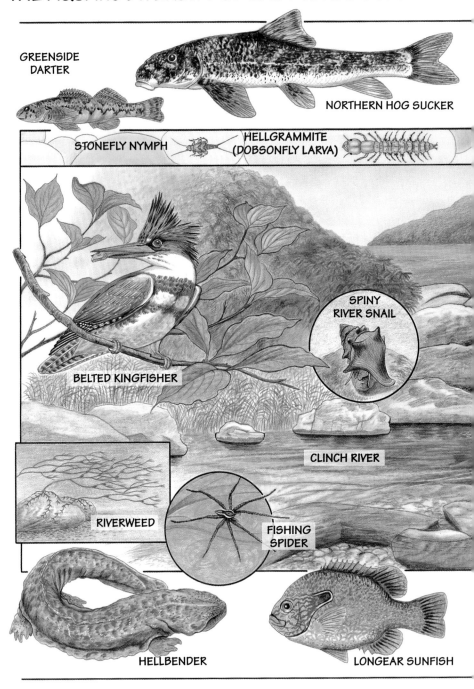

GREENSIDE DARTER

NORTHERN HOG SUCKER

STONEFLY NYMPH

HELLGRAMMITE (DOBSONFLY LARVA)

BELTED KINGFISHER

SPINY RIVER SNAIL

CLINCH RIVER

RIVERWEED

FISHING SPIDER

HELLBENDER

LONGEAR SUNFISH

The free-flowing rivers of East Tennessee contain the most diverse freshwater fish and mussel species in North America today. In fact, almost 300 kinds of fish live in the state because of its variety of aquatic habitats. Over time, each species has evolved a unique shape, color, and set of behaviors to help it survive.

Aquatic plants and invertebrates such as snails, insect nymphs and larvae

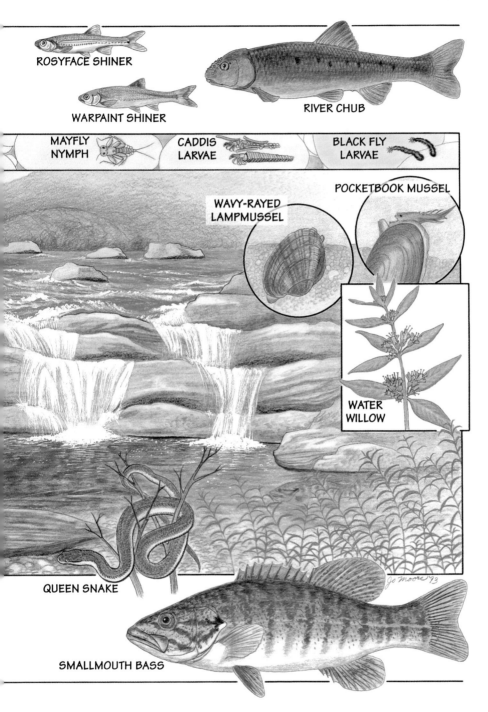

ROSYFACE SHINER

WARPAINT SHINER

RIVER CHUB

MAYFLY NYMPH

CADDIS LARVAE

BLACK FLY LARVAE

POCKETBOOK MUSSEL

WAVY-RAYED LAMPMUSSEL

WATER WILLOW

QUEEN SNAKE

SMALLMOUTH BASS

thrive in clean, silt-free water, forming a food base for fish and hellbender salamanders. The fish become meals for belted kingfishers and watersnakes. Examples of quality riverine habitats in East Tennessee may be seen at sites 45, 51, and 63 in this guide.

63 CHEROKEE NATIONAL FOREST: CONASAUGA RIVER

Description: *UNDERWATER VIEWING.* Springing from the rain-soaked slopes of the Southern Appalachians, this relatively silt-free stretch of the Conasauga State Scenic River supports over sixty fish species, including the federally-listed blue shiner, amber darter, and Conasauga logperch, as well as the state-listed trispot and coldwater darters. An exceptionally diverse community of mussels is also present.

Viewing Information: Equipped with mask and snorkel and a field guide to freshwater fishes, identifying these secretive and colorful fish will challenge adventuresome viewers. The Conasauga River Trail offers easy walking to river access points downstream from parking area. Snorkel in still, deep pools to view turtles, redeye bass, and sunfish; or kneel in shallow riffles to see Alabama hogsuckers, stonerollers, and male darters in breeding color. Check the downstream sides of boulders, rock crevices, and clumps of river weed. Best viewing on weekdays during warm months, when no rain has fallen in several days. *ALWAYS SNORKEL WITH A PARTNER AND WEAR SAFETY FLOTATION GEAR. ROADS MAY BE MUDDY AFTER HARD RAINS. PLEASE DO NOT DISTURB OR COLLECT THE SENSITIVE FAUNA OF THIS RIVER.*

Directions: *From junction of US 64 and US 411 south of Benton, travel south 6.7 miles on US 411, tuning left onto TN 313 (Ladd Springs Road, becomes Willis Springs Road). Travel four miles, then bear right on gravel Forest Service Road 221 (Pea Vine/Sheeds Creek Road). Continue for 4.7 miles and turn right into parking area for Conasauga River Trail 61; easy walking downstream.*

Ownership: USFS (615) 338-5201; TDEC/SRP (615) 532-0034
Size: Five river miles   **Closest Town:** Benton

Fish are naturally curious and will approach underwater viewers. The colorful darters and other fish native to the Conasauga River provide ideal viewing for those willing to don mask and snorkel.   J.R. SHUTE

Description: More than ninety percent of the Hiwassee River's 750,000-acre watershed is forested, contributing to exceptional aquatic wildlife diversity. Endangered mussels and over sixty-five species of fish thrive here, along with state-listed hellbender salamanders, easily seen resting on flat rocks. Watch for ruby-throated hummingbirds hovering over cardinal flowers and jewelweed. Mink, raccoon, osprey, great blue herons, and watersnakes thrive here. Beaver activity is easily seen along the John Muir National Recreation Trail.

Viewing Information: Stop at state park office on-site (open weekdays) or Forest Service office in Etowah (open Mon-Sat, April-November) for information on river access, raft rentals, etc. View from Cherokee National Forest roads, trails, or a river float trip May through September. One river section features Class I and II whitewater; previous experience best. Section between US 411 bridge and McClary Bend or Old Patty Bridge offers a quiet float. Weekend crowds June through August. Check water levels before planning float; best when at least two generators operating. *ALWAYS WEAR FLOTATION GEAR. OBEY ALL SAFETY REGULATIONS. WATER LEVELS FLUCTUATE QUICKLY; USE CAUTION WHEN WADING IN RIVER. RESPECT RIGHTS OF PRIVATE LANDOWNERS ALONG BANKS OF THE RIVER.*

Directions: *From Etowah, travel six miles south on US 411 to Hiwassee River bridge. State Park office located on southwest side of US 411 bridge over Hiwassee River, open weekdays.*

Ownership: TDEC/BPR (615) 338-4133; USFS (615) 263-5486; PVT
Size: Twenty-two State Scenic River miles; nine river miles PVT
Closest Town: Benton, Etowah

The clear running water and large rocks of the Hiwassee River provide habitat for the hellbender, North America's largest salamander, as well as endangered mussels and more than sixty-five species of fish.

STATE OF TENNESSEE:
TOURIST DEVELOPMENT

65 CHEROKEE NATIONAL FOREST: TELLICO AUTO LOOP

Description: Climbing from elevations of 1,000 to over 5,000 feet, this driving tour skirts wilderness, managed forest, and a black bear sanctuary. Excellent birding for many northern species near their southern range limits, such as black-capped chickadees, ravens, blackburnian warblers, veeries, and red-breasted nuthatches. Watch for the occasional bear, introduced European boar, red squirrels or "boomers," eastern chipmunk, and red or gray fox.

Viewing Information: Stop at Forest Service office on Tellico River for maps and information. Potential stops include many hiking trails; a three-mile loop hiking/biking trail at Indian Boundary Lake; or pull-offs along the Tellico River Road. The grassy bald at Whigg Meadow is home to the endangered Carolina northern flying squirrel and the state's smallest mammal, the pygmy shrew. Check high elevation forests for black-throated blue warblers, solitary vireo, and rose-breasted grosbeak during spring migration and summer. *NORTH RIVER ROAD IS GRAVEL, ROUGH AND WINDING, INACCESSIBLE TO RVs. AREA OPEN TO HUNTING IN SEASON; USE CAUTION. ROADS AT HIGHEST ELEVATIONS MAY BE CLOSED IN WINTER.*

Directions: *From junction of TN 68 and TN 165 in Tellico Plains, travel east on TN 165 through town; bear right to remain on TN 165 East. To reach Forest Service office, bear right at Oosterneck Creek. Tour continues on TN 165 for twenty-one miles to Stratton Gap. Turn left, cross under bridge and continue southwest on gravel Forest Service Road 217 (North River Road) for 1.1 miles. Bear right to continue on North River Road for 11.1 miles. Right on Tellico River Road to return to Tellico Plains.*

Ownership: USFS (615) 253-2520
Size: Thirty-seven miles (2.5-hour drive)   **Closest Town:** Tellico Plains

Five black bear sanctuaries, established on the Cherokee National Forest and the Great Smoky Mountains National Park in cooperation with TWRA, offer refuge especially to females during the hunting season.
BILL LEA

66 CHOTA PENINSULA OF TELLICO LAKE WMA

Description: Once the capital of the Cherokee Indian Nation, Chota Peninsula today provides ideal conditions for wintering waterfowl, including geese, mallards, wigeons, scaup, loons, and horned grebes. Also watch for migratory osprey, double-crested cormorant, and black tern in spring and fall. Ringed-billed gulls common in winter. Year-round, view white-tailed deer, wild turkey, and muskrat. Secretive rails and sedge and marsh wrens inhabit wet areas.

Viewing Information: View from Tanasi Memorial, or Chota Memorial at end of road. Refuge accessed by gravel road to right during open seasons. *REFUGE AREA CLOSED MID-OCTOBER THROUGH MID-FEBRUARY. USE CAUTION DURING SMALL GAME HUNTING SEASONS.*

Directions: *From US 411 in Vonore, travel south on TN 360 (Citico Road) for 7.4 miles. At that point, where TN 360 turns right, continue straight. Travel five miles and turn left at sign to Tellico Lake Wildlife Area, Chota Refuge Unit.*

Ownership: TVA (800) TVA-LAND; managed in cooperation with TWRA (615) 884-6767 and Ducks Unlimited (901) 758-3825
Size: 500 acres   **Closest Town:** Vonore

67 FORT LOUDOUN DAM - TELLICO DAM RESERVATION

Description: Fish stunned by their passage through the Fort Loudoun Dam powerhouse become easy prey for water birds at this site. Dozens of black-crowned night herons are joined by osprey May through October. Look for three species of gull in winter, and great blue heron and belted kingfisher year-round. Cottontail rabbits, white-tailed deer, and muskrats common year-round; prothonotary warblers nest May through August. Site of landmark court case involving the snail darter, an endangered fish.

Viewing Information: Black-crowned night herons most abundant below the dam, as are barn and cliff swallows and purple martins. Canada geese, wood ducks, double-crested cormorants, and loons seen from banks of canal along Little Tennessee River.

Directions: *From Interstate 75, take exit 81 (Lenoir City). Travel three miles north on US 321N and turn right into Lenoir City Park. Follow "River Bank Parking" signs to see black-crowned night herons. Back on US 321N, proceed 1.2 miles farther across Fort Loudoun Dam. Bear right to Tellico Parkway. Continue straight through stop sign to canal parking. Fort Loudoun Lock parking reached by an immediate right turn.*

Ownership: TVA (800) TVA-LAND; park leased to Lenoir City
Size: 579 acres   **Closest Town:** Lenoir City

68 FOOTHILLS PARKWAY (WESTERN SECTION)

Description: One of the best areas in Tennessee to consistently view large numbers of migratory raptors and perching birds in migration, March-May and September-October. Site of a state one-day high of 5,500 broad-winged hawks; 1,500 blue jays in four hours; and 1,500 common nighthawks in a single hour. It is common to see 1,000 raptors in a single day during autumn, including the peregrine falcon. Wildflowers bloom in spring, including flame azaelea, mountain laurel, bloodroot, and trailing arbutus; in fall, a splash of colorful asters.

Viewing Information: Binoculars and spotting scopes are necessities here. View from numerous pull-outs. Soaring ravens appear fall, winter, spring. By visiting in season, and with careful searching, twenty-five species of warblers may be seen in one day during migration. Large concentrations of monarch butterflies are possible mid-late September. Watch for white-tailed deer, small mammals, and the occasional river otter along Abrams Creek near western terminus. Try the 0.5-mile trail to Look Rock observation tower for ruffed grouse. Maps available at Great Smoky Mountains National Park (Site 71).

Directions: *From Maryville, follow US 321N seventeen miles through Walland to eastern terminus.*

Ownership: NPS (615) 436-1200
Size: Seventeen miles
Closest Town: Walland

The Look Rock observation tower offers spectacular views of the Great Smoky Mountains to the east, and often the chance to observe soaring ravens in spring, summer and fall or birds of prey in migration.
STATE OF TENNESSEE: TOURIST DEVELOPMENT

69 IJAMS NATURE CENTER-EASTERN STATE WMA

Description: WOA. Meadows, upland hardwood forest, sinkholes, and a spring-fed pond encircled by a boardwalk, all skirting an urban section of Fort Loudoun Lake, are magnets for wildlife and viewers alike. Landscaping for wildlife, a butterfly garden, and trails augment the educational offerings at this non-profit center. Flying squirrels are a year-round draw, along with deermice, pileated woodpeckers, and wood ducks. Migratory songbirds such as the ruby-throated hummingbird and orchard oriole appear in season. Adjacent Eastern State WMA offers views of occasional barn owls, snipe, and soras.

Viewing Information: Interpretive center offers maps, species lists, newsletter, and activities such as guided tours, including a popular program to view woodcock courtship flights at Eastern State WMA in March. On-site viewing from extensive trail system. Short braille trail. No facilities at WMA. *USE CAUTION WHILE VIEWING ON WMA DURING STATEWIDE HUNTING SEASONS; CONTACT TWRA TO DETERMINE DATES.*

Directions: *From Interstate 40 in Knoxville take Business Loop, exit 388A. Travel about 0.2 miles and take Cumberland Avenue exit. At top of hill turn left onto Gay Street, crossing Gay Street bridge. Continue straight through signal onto Sevier Street. At third signal, continue straight onto Island Home Avenue, and follow signs to Ijams Nature Center; entrance on left. To reach Eastern State WMA, contine on Island Home for 0.6 miles, turn left on McLure Lane, travel 0.3 miles and turn right at sign into gravel parking area.*

Ownership: City of Knoxville, operated by Ijams Nature Center Inc. (615) 577-4717; TWRA (615) 587-7037 or (800) 332-0900
Size: Ijams Nature Center eighty acres; Eastern State WMA 350 acres
Closest Town: Knoxville

The stunning spicebush swallowtail is named for the aromatic, lemon-scented host plants preferred by its larval, or caterpillar stage, including the native spicebush, sassafras and the bays.

BARBARA GERLACH

70 SHARPS RIDGE

Description: WOA. Sharps Ridge is easily accessed and has become a focal point for observing bird migrations. In-season visits may yield sightings of over thirty warbler species, including the Cape May, bay-breasted, and black-poll, as well as thrushes and tanagers. 150 species of birds recorded here.

Viewing Information: Seasonal viewing in April, May, September and October. Arrive in early morning, utilize public parking, and walk along the 1.3-mile ridgetop road. Knoxville Chapter of the Tennessee Ornithological Society offers a checklist and guided trips during migration seasons, and in conjunction with the Dogwood Arts Festival in mid-late April. *VISIT IN SMALL GROUPS. RESPECT RIGHTS OF PRIVATE LANDOWNERS.*

Directions: *From junction of US 441 and Interstate 640 in Knoxville, travel south on US 441 about one mile and turn west on Ludlow Avenue. Continue about 0.4 mi, turning right at the "Y" in the road and proceed up onto the ridge. Bear left (west) at the gap in the ridge. Road follows the ridgetop.*

Ownership: PVT; City of Knoxville, Department of Parks and Recreation (615) 521-2090
Size: 1.3 miles   **Closest Town:** Knoxville

71 GREAT SMOKY MOUNTAINS NATIONAL PARK

Description: WOA. The exceptional diversity of plant and animal communities here includes exquisite cove forests. Reintroduction of the red wolf, one of North America's most endangered carnivores, is underway; wolf sightings are unlikely. Park is a black bear sanctuary; sightings are possible spring through fall. A great variety of salamanders may be seen here, including the spring, slimy, and zigzag.

Viewing Information: Crowds of visitors Memorial Day through Labor Day, and during fall color season cause traffic conjestion. Sites of particular note are Cades Cove and Clingmans Dome, the highest point in the state at 6,643 feet. Over 800 miles of hiking trails; seventy-one miles of the Appalachian Trail. Wild turkey, white-tailed deer, and striped skunk common year-round. Visitor centers offer a wildlife map, checklists, and specific viewing information.

Directions: *Reached south of Interstate 40 by several routes. Usually accessed within Tennessee via US 321 from Maryville, US 441 from Gatlinburg.*

Ownership: NPS (615) 436-1200
Size: 520,004 acres; 245,109 acres in Tennessee
Closest Town: Gatlinburg in Tennessee, Cherokee in North Carolina

NEOTROPICAL MIGRANT BIRDS:
WORLD TRAVELERS IN TENNESSEE

SUMMER

WINTER

The scarlet tanager summers and nests in Tennessee, then migrates non-stop for several days across the Gulf of Mexico to spend winter in the forests of South America. The male tanager's plumage changes color from scarlet to olive green (see above) to complement his needs for each season.

Millions of thrushes, warblers, vireos, and flycatchers complete a similar journey twice each year. These birds are "neotropical migrants." They depend on habitats in two different areas of the world, and also need important resting areas along coastlines.

Neotropical bird populations are declining, and the reasons for this are not yet clear. The solution may lie in conserving large intact forests, both young and old, and practicing sustainable use on forest lands. Support the Tennessee Ornithological Society and natural resource agencies in their efforts to learn more about neotropical migrants.

72 PANTHER CREEK STATE PARK

Description: Stargazing minnows and eastern mystery snails await visitors to these limestone habitats along the banks of Panther Creek and Cherokee Lake. Watch for wild turkey, ruffed grouse, and bobwhite quail. Winter waterfowl are abundant, particularly pied-billed grebes, Canada geese, and coots. White-tailed deer and small mammals are common. Occasional winter bald eagles and summer osprey. Painted and spiny softshell turtles inhabit wetlands.

Viewing Information: An evening walk or drive on the main park road offers a high probability of viewing white-tailed deer, skunk, and opossum year-round. Six miles of trails feature Trout Walk and dramatic limestone sinks; Forest and Field Wildlife Trail under construction. Watch for small mammals, songbirds, and a variety of snakes. Park office offers maps, brochures.

Directions: *From junction of US 25E and US 11E in Morristown, travel south on US 11E for 7.7 miles. Turn right (west) on TN 342 (Panther Creek Road). Travel 2.4 miles to park entrance on right.*

Ownership: TDEC/BPR (615) 587-7046
Size: 1,435 acres **Closest Town:** Morristown

73 CHEROKEE NATIONAL FOREST: WEAVER'S BEND

Description: Floodplain forests and fields along the French Broad River attract yellow-throated warblers, swamp sparrows, and yellow-breasted chats. White-tailed deer are common, as are opossum and skunk; raccoon, fox, and weasel are uncommon. Wood ducks and fish may be seen from a canoe or raft.

Viewing Information: Primitive road around perimeter of area. Access by several trails, including the Chimney Rocks Trail from Paint Rock. High probability of seeing white-tailed deer outside hunting season. Rough-winged swallows and woodcock present in spring; common snipe in winter; great blue heron year-round. Bullfrogs noisy on summer nights. *USE CAUTION DURING HUNTING SEASONS, ESPECIALLY BIG GAME SEASON IN FALL; CONTACT USFS FOR DATES, WEAR BLAZE ORANGE. WEAR FLOTATION ON RIVER.*

Directions: *From junction with US 321 North in Newport, travel east on US 25-70 sixteen miles to Weavers Bend Road. Turn left and continue 3.2 miles to Forest Service Road 209C. Turn right and travel 1.6 miles to parking area. Boat access, outfitters in Hot Springs, NC; take-out on US 25-70 near Weavers Bend Road turn.*

Ownership: USFS (615) 638-4109
Size: Sixty acres **Closest Town:** Newport

Description: WOA. The expansive mudflats, freshwater marsh, and quiet sloughs adjacent to Douglas Reservoir provide spectacular shorebird viewing during fall migration, July-October. Watch for pectoral, least, semipalmated, and western sandpipers. Also common in late summer and fall are great egrets, and little blue, great blue and black-crowned night herons. Scan wet fields and thickets for nesting songbirds, including common yellowthroat, red-winged blackbird, and yellow warblers. Waterfowl and bald eagles visit in winter, as do song, swamp and savannah sparrows, northern harriers, and short-eared owls. White-tailed deer may be seen on wetland edges morning and evening.

Viewing Information: No facilities. Roadside viewing with spotting scope and binoculars. Visitors can also walk along shoreline or view from boat. *MUDDY ROAD CONDITIONS FOLLOWING HEAVY RAINS; WHEN IN DOUBT, WALK. EXERCISE CAUTION DURING STATEWIDE HUNTING SEASONS LATE AUGUST-FEBRUARY; CONTACT TWRA FOR DATES.*

Directions: *From Interstate 81 take exit 81 (Morristown/Newport). Travel 8.1 miles south on US 25E. Turn left on Rankin Hill Road and travel 3.8 miles. Turn left on Hill Road at bottom of hill, and travel straight on paved, then gravel Hill Road approximately 2.6 miles to historic coal tipple. Hill Road parallels, then crosses railroad tracks when approaching site.*

Ownership: TVA (800) TVA-LAND; leased to
TWRA (615) 587-7037 or (800)332-0900
Size: 740 acres   **Closest Town:** Newport

The frozen stance and blue-gray coloration of the great blue heron help this wading bird blend into its wetland surroundings. Herons wait patiently for a fish or frog to wander within range of their stiletto bill.

BILL LEA

89

75 BAYS MOUNTAIN PARK

Description: WOA. The rugged upland hardwood forests of this site are home to the gray squirrel, ruffed grouse, great horned owl, whip-poor-will, and reptiles, including the copperhead and black rat snake, and fence lizard. Cove hardwoods attract ovenbirds, scarlet tanagers, white-tailed deer, gray fox, and salamanders. Lake and pond habitats offer chances to view beaver, muskrat, wood ducks, snapping and painted turtles, bullfrogs, freshwater jellyfish, and smallmouth bass. More than 190 species of birds have been observed here.

Viewing Information: High probability of seeing birds such as the yellow-billed cuckoo, worm-eating warbler, and wood thrush May through July. Great blue and green-backed herons may be viewed year-round, along with white-tailed deer, woodchuck, and eastern chipmunk. Watch for wild turkey and ring-necked duck in winter. Bobcat, weasel, and osprey are more elusive. Nature center has information for guided and self-guided tours, including popular pontoon boat tours. Primitive group camping by reservation only. Nearby Meadowview Marsh offers patient viewers a chance to see secretive American and least bitterns, also Virginia rails in tiny freshwater wetland.

Directions: *From Interstate 81, take exit 57B (Kingsport) onto Interstate 181. Travel 4.5 miles to exit 51 and proceed straight through traffic signal (becomes Wilcox Drive).* **Bays Mountain:** *travel 0.6 miles and turn left on Reservoir Road. Travel 2.8 miles and turn right on Bays Mountain Road. Travel 0.2 miles and bear left. Follow signs to park.* **Meadowview Marsh:** *travel 0.8 miles and turn left into gravel pullout. Through fence and to left to reach marsh trails.*

Ownership: City of Kingsport (615) 229-9447;
Meadowview Marsh: Eastman Chemical Company (615) 229-3317
Size: 3,000 acres **Closest Town:** Kingsport

Eastern cottontails may produce four litters of up to nine young in a single year. Predators help to keep these populations from outgrowing their available habitat.
JOHN NETHERTON

Description: WOA. The large, intact forests of Steele Creek Park and the Slagle Hollow Natural Area provide vital nesting habitat for Neotropical migrant songbirds, such as the Acadian flycatcher, worm-eating warbler, Louisiana waterthrush, and scarlet tanager. Watch for mallards, gadwalls and pied-billed grebes on the fifty-three-acre lake in winter; during summer, green-backed and yellow-crowned night herons may be seen, with wood ducks year-round. Osprey visits each spring.

Viewing Information: Key point to visit astride Tennessee-Virginia state line. Numerous guided activities, information on trails offered through nature center. Natural area may be accessed through Slagle Hollow Trail. Spring signals blooming painted trillium and turk's-cap lily, and arrival of migrant birds.

Directions: From Interstate 81, exit 74A (U.S. Hwy 11W north, Bristol). Follow U.S. 11W north 2.4 mi and turn right onto TN 126 west. Travel 1.1 miles, turning left at sign to Steele Creek Park. Turn right and cross bridge; entrance gate is 0.4 mile on left.

Ownership: City of Bristol (615) 764-4023
Size: 2,196 acres   **Closest Town:** Bristol

From a crouch, the red fox may spring up to fifteen feet to land with forepaws pinning down an unsuspecting mouse or frog.   LEONARD LEE RUE III

77 CHEROKEE NATIONAL FOREST: LITTLE OAK WATCHABLE WILDLIFE AREA

Description: A stop on the Watauga Ranger District's Flatwoods Auto Tour, this site is tucked away in the popular Little Oak Recreation Area on the shores of South Holston Lake. Two interpretive trails offer views of white-tailed deer, ruffed grouse, wild turkeys, pileated woodpeckers, and an occasional timber rattlesnake, which should be observed from a safe distance.

Viewing Information: The 1.5-mile Little Oak Mountain Trail crosses through cove and upland hardwood forest and forest openings created to attract wildlife; also featured are an animal tracking pit and vistas of the lake. The Little Oak Trail follows the lakeshore, with views of Holston Mountain. A wildlife photography blind, native wildflower and grass plantings, and nest boxes are planned for this area. Watch for the occasional common loon, grebe, and three species of gull in winter. Also the site of a bald eagle hacking project; please heed posted warnings to protect eaglets. Contact USFS office for Auto Tour brochures and maps. *USE CAUTION WHEN HIKING DURING FALL HUNTING SEASONS; CONTACT USFS FOR SEASON DATES, LOCATIONS.*

Directions: *From Bristol, take US 421 south twelve miles to Camp Tom Howard/ Flatwoods Road (Forest Service Road 87). Turn right, travel eight miles to "Three Rocks," at junction of Forest Service Roads 87 and 87G. Turn right on FS Road 87G and proceed 1.3 miles to recreation area.*

Ownership: USFS (615) 542-2942
Size: 260 acres   **Closest Town:** Bristol

The song of the upland chorus frog sounds like a thumbnail running along the teeth of a comb. In the South, these frogs start singing in late winter during cool rains.
JACK DERMID

78 WILBUR LAKE

Description: WOA. Sheltered by bluffs along the middle stretch of the Watauga River, Wilbur Lake does not freeze in winter and offers resting and feeding habitat for waterfowl, including ring-necked ducks and buffleheads. Waterfowl rarities sighted here include the oldsquaw, and white-winged and surf scoter. Waterfowl aggregations attract raptors, particularly Cooper's hawks. Listen for the slap of a beaver's tail on the water after dusk.

Viewing Information: Songbird viewing productive year-round; try the picnic area for ovenbird, Louisiana waterthrush, and hooded warbler in early summer. Ruffed grouse forage early mornings or late afternoons near rhododendron thickets. Watch the roadsides for woodchucks. Camping, hiking on Cherokee National Forest. Appalachian Trail crosses nearby Watauga Dam.

Directions: *From Elizabethton, travel 0.6 miles south on US 321. Turn left onto Siam Road. Bear left at 3.5 miles to stay on Siam; continue 0.6 miles and turn right on Wilbur Dam Road. Travel 1.8 miles. Parking, picnic areas beyond dam.*

Ownership: TVA (800) TVA-LAND; USFS (615) 542-2942
Size: Seventy-five acres   **Closest Town:** Elizabethton

79 ERWIN NATIONAL FISH HATCHERY - UNICOI COUNTY HERITAGE MUSEUM

Description: WOA. Located on fish hatchery grounds, this mature forest features some trees over 300 years old. The forest, along with adjacent city park ponds and an easy self-guided walking trail, offer wildlife viewing and education. Osprey and waterfowl, including mallards, pied-billed grebes, redheads, and blue-winged teal visit ponds during migration. In warmer months, experience the sights and sounds of spring peepers, chorus, green and wood frogs. Watch for ringneck and garter snakes.

Viewing Information: Pick up a self-guided audio tape at museum (variable schedule May 1 - October 1 only) or brochure at fish hatchery (open seven days) to visit Pat Alderman Nature Trail. Songbird viewing in spring and summer, wildflowers in spring. Listen for grouse drumming winter and spring.

Directions: *From Interstate 181 south of Johnson City, take exit 19 (Erwin). Cross over interstate and turn left onto US 19-23 at signal. Fish hatchery entrance is on left, museum and nature trail adjacent.*

Ownership: USFWS (615) 743-4712; Unicoi County Heritage Museum (615) 743-9449
Size: Thirty acres   **Closest Town:** Erwin

80 CHEROKEE NATIONAL FOREST: UNAKA MOUNTAIN AUTO TOUR

Description: This 3.5-hour auto tour loops through the Unaka Range of the Southern Appalachians, climbing from 2,000 to 5,000 feet in elevation through managed forest and designated wilderness. Travel through the dense rhododendron and hemlocks of Rock Creek, listening for black-throated green and Swainson's warblers, and Louisiana waterthrush. Next visit grassy balds at the Beauty Spot, home to least weasels, New England cottontail rabbits, bobcats, barred owls, and snow buntings. The drive climbs to misty mountaintop "islands" of red spruce, with pigmy and Yonahlassee salamanders, saw-whet owls, and magnolia warblers. Soaring ravens and occasional peregrine falcons may be seen at Unaka Mountain Overlook.

Viewing Information: Auto tour brochure and birding information available at Forest Service office in Erwin, open weekdays. Appalachian Trail accessible from auto route. Outstanding birding for black-throated blue and Canada warblers spring through fall. Year-round, look for golden-crowned kinglets and red-breasted nuthatches. Black bear and red fox may be seen occasionally. *RVs DISCOURAGED DUE TO NARROW, WINDING GRAVEL ROADS. PREPARE FOR HIGH WINDS AND SUDDEN WEATHER CHANGES AT HIGHER ELEVATIONS ANY TIME OF YEAR. ROADS MAY BE CLOSED SEASONALLY FOR SNOW AND ICE. REMOTE AREA.* Last stop on tour is Site 79.

Directions: *From Interstate 181 south of Johnson City, take exit 19 (Erwin). Cross over interstate, turning right on Main Street. Forest Service office is 0.4 miles on right. Tour follows TN 395 east, Forest Service Road 230, and TN 107 west.*

Ownership: USFS (615) 743-4452
Size: Thirty-one-mile loop drive (allow 3.5 hours)
Closest Town: Erwin

High in the mountains of east Tennessee, on the cold nights of early spring, listen for the "two-stones-clicking" call of the courting male saw-whet owl. The first nest recorded in the state was documented on the Cherokee National Forest in the spring of 1992.

FRED J. ALSOP III

Description: The Roan massif soars to over 6,200 feet, robed in misty forests of stunted buckeye and beech trees, and gardens of purple rhododendron. Wind-blown grassy balds are havens for rare plants, where ravens cavort in the fierce updrafts. More than 150 species of birds present including least and alder flycatchers, veeries, chestnut-sided warblers, and saw-whet owls. Conifer trees attract pine siskins, red crossbills, and evening grosbeaks in winter. Red squirrels are present year-round. Carolina juncos (known as "snowbirds" to Southerners) are also common. Endangered northern flying squirrels and rare New England cottontails are near their southeastern range limits here.

Viewing Information: State Park Visitor Center offers maps, brochures, programs, activities, and services. Forest Service offers maps and barrier-free access through spruce-fir forest and rhododendron. *PLEASE REMAIN ON TRAILS TO PROTECT SENSITIVE PLANTS. PREPARE FOR SUDDEN WEATHER CHANGES AT HIGHER ELEVATIONS AT ANY TIME OF YEAR. ROADS CLOSED SEASONALLY DUE TO SNOW AND ICE. TRAFFIC CONGESTION AT PEAK RHODODENDRON BLOOMS MID-JUNE, AND DURING AUTUMN COLOR IN OCTOBER.*

Directions: *From Elizabethton, travel eighteen miles south on US 19E. Turn south on TN 143 at village of Roan Mountain. Travel three miles to state park visitor center. Forest Service office located off-site on Main Street in Erwin, accessed from exit 19 of Interstate 181 south of Johnson City. Open weekdays.*

Ownership: TDEC/BPR (615) 772-3303; USFS (615) 743-4452; Southern Appalachian Highlands Conservancy (615) 434-2555
Size: state park 2,100 acres; national forest 2,900 acres
Closest Town: Roan Mountain, Elizabethton

Hikers in spruce-fir forests will hear the drawn-out, scolding trill of the red squirrel. Surprisingly tame and very agile, red squirrels devour conifer seeds, leaving only remnants of cones to mark their favorite feeding spots.
JOHN GERLACH

95

WILDLIFE INDEX

This index identifies some of the more interesting, uncommon, or popular wildlife found in Tennessee and some of the best sites for viewing selected species. The numbers following each species refer to viewing sites.

INSECTS

Butterflies 11, 30, 53, 68, 69

Cave glowworms 44

FISH

Coldwater fish 43, 64, 65, 71, 79

Warmwater fish 24, 45, 48, 51, 63, 64

AMPHIBIANS AND REPTILES

Frogs 1, 48, 79

Lizards 15, 32

Salamanders 44, 50, 64, 65, 71, 80

Snakes 1, 5, 36, 37, 64

Turtles 1, 4, 7, 11, 21, 31, 46

BIRDS

Bald eagle 1, 19, 22, 43

Barred owl 1, 4, 9, 34, 59

Black-crowned night heron 33, 34, 67

Black-necked silt 12

Common raven 65, 68, 71, 80, 81

Great blue heron 1, 22, 35, 74

Great egret 1, 5, 20, 74

Least tern 1, 6, 8, 9, 12

Marsh birds 14, 22, 28, 46, 66

Mississippi kite 1, 2, 6, 7, 8, 9, 11

Northern bobwhite 16, 17, 18, 22, 25

Osprey 22, 54

Peregrine falcon 68, 80, 81

Raptors (in migration) 53, 58, 60, 68, 81

Ruffed grouse 45, 51, 65, 72, 75, 77, 80

Sandhill cranes 55

BIRDS (cont)

Shorebirds 1, 12, 18, 48, 52, 74

Vultures, turkey and black 39, 40

Waterfowl (wintering)—ducks, geese, loons, cormorants 1, 3, 6, 20, 22, 55, 66

Wild turkey 6, 7, 9, 13, 19, 51

Wood duck 1, 5, 13, 73

Woodland songbirds 1, 6, 9, 19, 30, 47, 50, 65, 68, 70, 71, 81

MAMMALS

Bats 57

Beaver 1, 4, 13, 27, 33, 46, 64,78

Bison 19

Black bear 65, 71, 80

Flying squirrels:
  Southern 59, 69
  Northern 65, 71, 81

Foxes:
  Gray 17, 38, 50
  Red 1, 8, 14, 18, 22

Fox squirrel 7, 16

Gray Squirrel 6, 19, 30, 51, 75

Raccoon 5, 7, 9, 13, 20

Red squirrel 65, 71, 80, 81

River otter 1, 5

Swamp rabbit 5, 6, 9, 13, 18

White-tailed deer 7, 9, 13, 16, 19, 23, 47, 51, 72

WILDFLOWERS

Spring-blooming wildflowers 21, 30, 42, 47, 62, 65, 71, 81